GRASSES AND
BAMBOOS

A PRACTICAL GUIDE

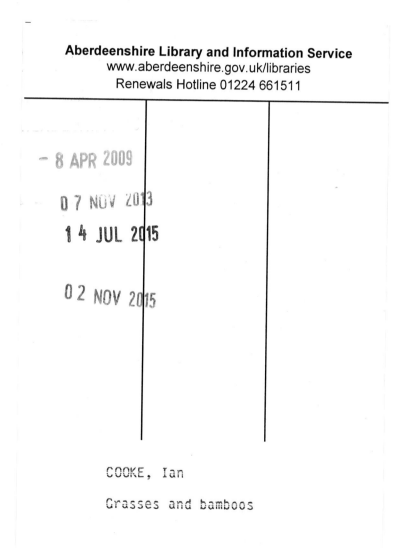

GRASSES AND
BAMBOOS
A PRACTICAL GUIDE

IAN COOKE

NEW
HOLLAND

This edition published in 2009 by
New Holland Publishers (UK) Ltd
London · Cape Town · Sydney · Auckland
www.newhollandpublishers.com

Garfield House
86–88 Edgware Road
London W2 2EA
United Kingdom

80 McKenzie Street
Cape Town 8001
South Africa

Unit 1, 66 Gibbes Street
Chatswood, NSW 2067
Australia

218 Lake Road
Northcote, Auckland
New Zealand

10 9 8 7 6 5 4 3 2 1

Text copyright © 2005 Ian Cooke
Illustration copyright © 2005 New Holland Publishers (UK) Ltd
Copyright © 2005 New Holland Publishers (UK) Ltd

ISBN 978 1 84773 338 2

Editor: Joanna Smith
Senior Editor: Clare Hubbard
Editorial Direction: Rosemary Wilkinson
Designer: Lisa Tai
Picture researcher: Ian Cooke
Illustrations: Coral Mula/Map: Bill Smuts
Production: Ben Byram-Wigfield

Reproduction by Pica Digital PTE Ltd, Singapore
Printed and bound by Times Offset (M) Sdn. Bhd., Malaysia

DISCLAIMER

The author and publishers have made every effort to ensure that
all instructions given in this book are safe and accurate, but they
cannot accept liability for any resulting injury or loss or damage
to either property or person, whether direct or consequential and
howsoever arising.

ACKNOWLEDGEMENTS

A particular thank you to Des Martin, owner of Mozart House
Nursery, for his assistance in the research for this book and to many
other nursery owners who sent me information. My appreciation
also goes to Tony Hallam for checking my manuscript and to my
partner Philip for his patience and encouragement.

PICTURE CREDITS

Ian Cooke: pages 5, 22, 28, 46, 50, 64, 70, 80, 84 *right*, 89 *centre*,
89 *right,* jacket back cover *top right.*

Photos Horticultural: jacket front cover *top right*, pages 7 (HDRA
Ryton Gdn), 8–9, 15, 16–17, 19, 26, 32–33, 40–41, 43, 44 (Beth
Chatto Gardens), 56 (Godstone Gardeners Club at Chelsea FS
2000), 58, 60 (Les Pre de Jerbourg), 72–73, 74, 86 *top,* 87 *top
right* (photographer MJK), 89 *left centre*, 90 *top right*, 91 *bottom.*

Derek St Romaine: jacket front cover *top left, bottom left, bottom
right,* pages 13, 14, 18, 21 (garden: Simon Huggins, Bridport,
Dorset), 23, 27 (designed by SpiderGarden.com), 29 (designed by
Patrick Wynniatt-Husey & Patrick), 37, 39, 42, 48, 52 (Simon
Huggins, Bridport, Dorset), 54, 62 (Beachcomber Trading Ltd), 66
(design by Liz Robinson), 68, 75, 76 (RHS Chelsea 1997, EMI A
Creative Century, designer David Stevens), 77 (garden: Robert van
den Hurk, design: Phil Nash), 78 (designed by Stephen
Woodhams), 79, 81 (RHS Chelsea 1997, Sparsholt College),
82–83, 84 *left* (Glen Chantry garden, Essex), 85 *top* (Glen Chantry
garden, Essex), 85 *bottom*, 86 *bottom*, 87 *top left*, 87 *bottom
centre*, 88 *top left*, 88 *right centre* (Glen Chantry garden, Essex), 90
top left, 91 *top*, jacket back cover *top left.*

Page 2 Yellow azaleas and golden-leaved Mexican orange
blossom contrast with ornamental grasses in this permanent
planting.

Page 5 Grasses provide the perfect contrast in colour and texture
to the flamboyant colours of herbaceous perennials.

Contents

Introduction

Fine foliage, architectural outlines, delicate flowers, summer colour and winter interest – ornamental grasses provide all this and more. In fact, grasses are truly wonderful plants which contribute to our landscapes throughout the world. Bamboos are actually woody grasses and all these comments equally apply to the amazing world of bamboos.

Grasses are the most important of all plant families. Among the grasses we have all the many cereal crops that provide a staple diet for most of the world's population, such as wheat, barley, oats, rice and maize. Grasses also supply food for many of the animals that provide us with meat and dairy products. Then there is sugar cane, a tropical grass and the source of much of our sugar. Grasses provide us with lawns, an invaluable living carpet within many landscapes, and a surface on which to play sports of all kinds, from bowls through to rugby.

Alongside these useful grasses, there are the villains, the many pernicious weeds we have in the grass family. Most gardeners will be familiar with the difficulty of eradicating problem grasses such as twitch. These plants give grasses a bad name and have led some gardeners to be hesitant about using ornamental grasses. Fortunately, the majority of ornamental grasses are well behaved and do not become troublemakers. In fact, most grasses are easy to grow, are undemanding of conditions and perform well in the first season. They do not require deadheading, staking or spraying. Most are hardy and typically perennial, performing reliably for many seasons in the garden.

Ornamental grasses do not have flowers which are as big or colourful as those of other garden plants such as roses and lilies. However, the flowers of many grasses are distinct in their own way and some grasses have brightly coloured foliage. The attraction of grasses is more subtle and the contribution they make to a garden more restrained. Each individual stem is delicate, soft and insubstantial, having little impact alone. However, an established clump has a strong vertical emphasis and will make an effective architectural statement. It is this combination of the strong and delicate that gives grasses their unique effect. The numerous small stems and leaves change constantly through the seasons, and as the wind blows they come to life, providing visual interest and gentle rustling sounds.

Add to this the effects of light on the shimmering foliage making a dynamic contribution to any landscape. A clump of grasses is rarely solid – the sun will shine through them, creating a myriad of different light and shade patterns which move with the breeze. Rain will inevitably cause the leaves to bow down and droplets of water will cascade from each leaf, adding further to the effect. And the gaunt skeletal remnants of stem and foliage linger throughout the winter months, to be brought to sparkling life by every winter frost.

This book is a general introduction to ornamental grasses and bamboos. I hope to enthuse you about these wonderful plants. I have described how to grow and propagate them, and suggested many imaginative ways to make the most of them in your garden.

Right Frosty mornings bring a bonus when the gaunt skeletons of last year's grasses come alive with a sparkling, jewel-like quality.

1 | A TOUCH OF BOTANY

Right The varying foliage colours of these ornamental grasses
show the wonderful diversity of this valuable group of plants.

Form and Function

Grasses belong to the plant family usually known as Graminae. The correct name is, in fact, Poaceae, but this name is less commonly used. Altogether there are around 620 genera and over 9000 species of grasses. In addition there are thousands of cultivars, or artificially bred named varieties. This is a large and very diverse group of plants, one of the largest plant families in the world.

All grasses are monocotyledonous plants, which means that when the seed germinates, they only produce one seed leaf. Most grasses are herbaceous perennials which grow from a clump, although some are creeping and spreading plants. All grasses are distinct in having hollow stems. Bamboos are the only woody members of the grass family and are grouped in Bambusoideae, a subdivision of the grass family. They are nevertheless still grasses.

GRASS FLOWERS

The flowers of many other plants are large as their purpose is to attract insects to pollinate them, leading to seed production and future generations. However, grasses depend on the wind for pollination so their flowers do not need to be showy or brightly coloured. Instead they have large numbers of very delicate flowers that move with the wind, dispersing and catching pollen.

Individual grass flowers are called florets and are clustered together in structures called inflorescences. These can be various different shapes, including spikes, racemes or panicles. Many grass flowers also have needle-like bristles, called awns, that extend out substantially, increasing the size of the flower-heads. It is often these awns that give grass flowers their very delicate appearance.

GRASS ROOTS

Grasses have the somewhat unwarranted reputation of being invasive and taking over the garden. This is not true for the majority of ornamental grasses. However, in order to avoid this problem we need to understand how grasses grow. Some stay in distinct tufts, slowly expanding over the years. These are the clump-formers and basically they will stay where you plant them.

Grasses that creep or spread produce vigorous growths that extend the plant much faster and colonize

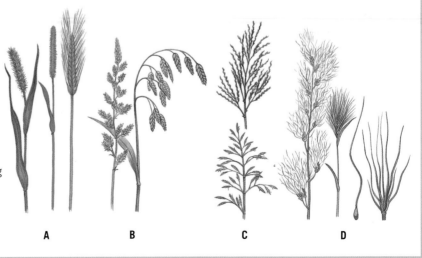

GRASS FLOWERS

The spike is the simplest type. It is narrow and unbranched, with flowers fixed directly to the stem. (A)

The raceme has flowers attached by short stems to the main stem. It flowers from the bottom upwards. (B)

The panicle has side branches that divide, giving a more complex and showy flower head. (C)

The awn is a needle-like structure that extends beyond the flower. (D)

A   B   C   D

GRASS ROOTS

A clump-forming grass such as
Festuca glauca. (A)

A creeping grass with stolons,
Agrostis stolonifera for example. (B)

A creeping grass with rhizomes such as
Phalaris arundinacea 'Picta'. (C)

new areas. They may do this by means of stolons which run above the ground, or rhizomes which grow beneath the soil. Obviously creeping grasses must be used with care, but they can be very useful in situations such as banks where they will stabilize the soil.

SEDGES, RUSHES AND CAT TAILS

Sedges, rushes and cat tails are closely related to the grasses. The following old garden rhyme may offer some easy ways of remembering the differences: "Sedges have edges and rushes are round; grasses are hollow and rush all around".

The sedge family, Cyperaceae, is a relatively small group of plants that often grow in damp or even wet conditions. Sedges are mostly quite small plants, often less than 30cm (12in) in height. They have solid triangular stems and the roots are usually rhizomatous.

Many of these plants have very attractive foliage, which is generally evergreen and often quite stiff in comparison to grasses. Most of the ornamental sedges that are regularly grown are within the genus *Carex* or *Cyperus*. Cotton grass (*Eriophorum angustifolium*) is also included here.

The rushes, Juncaceae, are another minor family with grass-like cylindrical leaves. They are true moisture-lovers and only flourish in very wet soil or actually growing in water. Their vertical habit contrasts well with the horizontal line of the water surface and they look good in formal ponds and water features. The rushes include the genera *Juncus* and *Luzula*.

The cat tails, Typhaceae, make up the smallest group of them all. They have narrow strap-like leaves and like to grow in very wet conditions. To add to the confusion, cat tails are also known as bulrushes or reedmaces. For ease, the term 'grasses' will be used to describe all these plants where generalized statements can be made.

SEDGES

True grasses have narrow leaves with long, straight veins. They have hollow cylindrical stems with nodes. (A)

Cat tails have narrow, flat, iris-like leaves and velvety brown, cigar-shaped flower structures. (B)

Rushes are grass-like plants with solid cylindrical stems without nodes. (C)

Sedges have triangular stems that are also solid and lack nodes. (D)

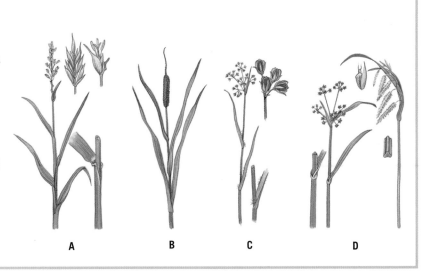

Grass Types

From tiny tufts through to lofty giants, there is a whole host of different grasses. The outlines of some, such as blue fescue (*Festuca glauca*) are tufted like leafy hedgehogs, whilst others, like the tender fountain grass (*Pennisetum setaceum*), have a looser, softer structure which makes them almost trailing. Yet others, such as switch grass (*Panicum virgatum*) are stiff and upright as if on parade.

The tallest grasses have strong vertical growth and provide a dramatic statement in any garden display. Some of the tall upright ones, such as the aristocratic giant reed (*Arundo donax*), have strong vertical stems and trailing foliage, which creates a waterfall effect. These varied characteristics mean that grasses can be used to create diverse effects in many situations in the garden.

GROWTH PATTERNS

Among the perennial grasses, there are two distinct growth patterns. Cool season grasses start growing actively in late winter and spring, and often flower in spring or early summer. Once temperatures rise and water becomes more restricted, they grow slowly or start to become dormant. Plants such as blue fescue (*Festuca glauca*) and Bowles' golden grass (*Milium effusum* 'Aureum') are cool season growers.

Warm season grasses thrive in the heat and do not start their growth cycles until late in the spring. Their peak display and flowering season will usually be late summer. Pampas grasses (*Cortaderia*), Japanese silver grasses (*Miscanthus*) and fountain grass (*Pennisetum setaceum*) are examples of warm season grasses.

FOLIAGE COLOUR

In essence, all grasses have leaves and contribute to the garden in some way, but many have more striking colours or shapes that make them especially interesting. The

---

GROWTH PATTERNS OF GRASSES

Tufted grasses have a rounded spiky shape. Examples include blue fescue (*Festuca glauca*). (A)

Arching grasses have gracefully curved foliage and sometimes flower stems. Examples include fountain grass (*Pennisetum setaceum*). (B)

Upright grasses have a strongly vertical emphasis and are generally taller than their width. Examples include switch grass (*Panicum virgatum*). (C)

Some grasses have a combination shape which is a mixture of types. Examples include Japanese silver grass (*Miscanthus sinensis*) or feather reed grass (*Calamagrostis* x *acutiflora*). (D)

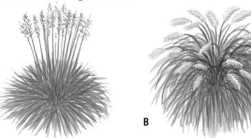

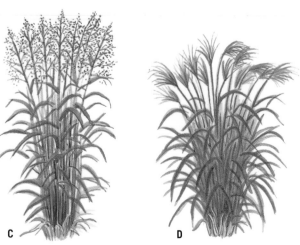

A   B   C   D

narrow linearity of the leaves gives grasses their individual value, which contrasts so well with the broad leaves and bold flowers of other plants. One value of foliage plants is their instant effect, almost from the moment of planting and throughout most of the season.

THE GREENS

The most common leaf colour is, of course, green and even without flowers, many green grasses are attractive. Ponytail grass (*Stipa tenuissima*) is a very delicate grass with fine, needle-thin green foliage. Hakone grass (*Hakonechloa macra*) has a weeping form with short green bamboo-like leaves making a tiny soft mound. Even with no difference in leaf colour, these two grasses alone have enough contrast and interest to be grown together. Green is, of course, a neutral colour and you can use as many green-leaved plants in a garden as you want without causing any discord.

THE BLUES

Blue is another common leaf colour among grasses, and it is usually a silvery blue of glaucous foliage with a slightly waxy finish. The most common blue grass is probably the tufty blue fescue (*Festuca glauca*), of which there are some fine modern selections such as 'Elijah Blue'. The invasive blue lyme grass (*Leymus arenarius*) is somewhat taller and should only be used where it can romp away harmlessly. Blue hair grass (*Koeleria glauca*), and blue oat grass (*Helictotrichon sempervirens*) also both have blue foliage.

VARIEGATION

As well as plain colours, grasses also come in jazzy variegated guises, with both silver and gold colourings. The white variegated types are very useful as they lighten up a planting scheme and can be used with any other colour combination. There are some very good variegated forms of Japanese silver grass (*Miscanthus sinensis*) such as 'Morning Light' with narrow leaves, and the more vigorous 'Cabaret'.

Yellow variegated grasses are probably the brightest of all and although very valuable in the garden, they need to be used with care and moderation. Too many yellow variegated leaves can look very garish and such foliage will not always complement other plants. One

Above The aptly named Japanese blood grass (*Imperata cylindrica* 'Rubra') gets better as the season progresses and the colour of the foliage deepens.

of the best is probably Bowles' golden sedge (*Carex elata* 'Aurea'), which is of particular value as it is evergreen. During the winter its pure gold foliage colour usually intensifies.

AND EVEN RED

Finally there are a couple of grasses with conspicuous red or purple foliage. Japanese blood grass (*Imperata cylindrica* 'Rubra'), makes a small plant with young yellowish-lime leaves tipped with red. As the season progresses, the colour intensifies and spreads over the entire leaf. By autumn the effect is an intense blood red.

My personal favourite is purple fountain grass (*Pennisetum setaceum* 'Rubrum'), which is widely grown in the USA. This beautiful plant is decked with rich burgundy foliage, topped at the end of the season with fluffy pink flower and seed heads. Sadly it is tender and will not survive frost. If available, it is worth growing as a summer ephemeral.

More Grass Types

The majority of grasses are grown for their foliage, however some are noted and bred for their attractive flowers. Most are perennial plants, but annual grasses also have a place in gardens as they can provide a stunning summer display in a matter of months. Here I also look at some of the lesser-known members of the grass family.

FLOWERING GRASSES

Most grasses will flower eventually but some have more spectacular flowers than others. In virtually all cases, the attraction of a grass flower is not its colour but more its form and structure. Most grass flowers have a very neutral colour, but this can be seen as an advantage as it enables us to associate them with so many other plants and colour combinations.

Grass flowers are also, almost without exception, very light, open structures and in a garden context we can usually see through them to plants behind. Quite spectacular effects can be created by using the see-through effect of grasses as a veil to partially mask the brighter colours behind. Equally, placing grasses where the light will filter through them offers another visual trick used by many creative gardeners.

Grass flowerheads vary in size, from the huge dense plumes of pampas grass (*Cortaderia selloana*) to the tiny delicate spikelets of switch grass (*Panicum virgatum*) or the tiny 'lockets' on the lesser quaking grass (*Briza minor*).

For grasses to be valuable as flowering specimens, they must perform reliably each season and deliver a profusion of good flower-heads. One of the most spectacular is Spanish oat grass (*Stipa gigantea*). It makes a low mound of dark foliage with huge golden flowerheads hovering in the air above. Pampas grass (*Cortaderia selloana*) is another stunning plant. It is available in tall and dwarf forms, both with magnificent feathery plumes in creamy white or sometimes dusky pink. Appearing in early autumn, the plumes will often last right through the winter.

There are many plants within the genus *Miscanthus* that have good flowers as well as foliage, although the flowers often have a slightly shaggy look. The flowers of switch grass (*Panicum virgatum* 'Rubrum') are so delicate as to give an almost transparent quality. The flowers of fountain grass (*Pennisetum alopecuroides*) are more substantial and look like small bottle brushes. They are heavy enough to make the stems bow attractively with their weight, giving the plant its common name.

Among the grasses we should not, of course, forget subjects such as the lesser bulrush (*Typha angustifolia*) whose immense and distinctive brown flower-heads can be seen above many streams in midsummer. Another

Above Being evergreen, the foliage of sedges adds colour and interest to the garden throughout the year.

moisture-lover is the common cotton grass (*Eriophorum angustifolium*) whose fluffy white flower-heads can often be seen in damp ground.

RUSHES AND SEDGES

In the garden, these grass-like plants achieve a very similar effect to grasses although they have particular values because of the situations in which they grow.

Among the rushes are plants that thrive in dry shady situations such as the common woodrush (*Luzula sylvatica*). The form 'Aurea' has splendid gold foliage whose colour intensifies with the winter cold. *Juncus* by contrast is at its best in a moist waterside location. The most curious of these is probably the corkscrew rush (*Juncus effusus spiralis*) which looks like a loose bundle of curly green garden wire.

Sedges need moist conditions so are best grown near water. Most make dense arching tufts or hummocks. One of the most familiar is *Carex morrowii* which is usually seen in its brightly variegated form called 'Evergold'. It is an excellent foliage plant and, being evergreen, adds a touch of winter sun to any garden. *Carex buchananii* has thin, almost hair-like, foliage in a soft brown. It is a curious plant and may not always be appreciated; in the wrong light it sometimes looks dead.

RESTIOS – SOMETHING NEW

Restios are evergreen rush-like plants, native mainly to South Africa and Australia. They have only recently become more widely grown and their culture is still a bit experimental but it looks as if they may soon be the new plants that everyone wants.

They vary considerably in appearance, some looking like grasses, others like bamboos or even horsetails. Typically they have striking foliage, creating a very dramatic and architectural effect. With all of them, male and female flowers are on separate plants. Most are quite upright in their habit of growth and have very small, much reduced leaves, giving them a sparse or feathery appearance.

Being quite new to cultivation, the hardiness of restios is not yet fully proven. It is generally a combination of cold and wet that they do not like. To be absolutely safe, treat them as tender perennials in temperate regions and overwinter in a frost-free greenhouse.

The South African broom reed (*Elegia capensis*) has attractive coppery sheaths on bright green stems and grows to 1.8m (6ft). At a glance it resembles a giant horsetail. It is said to be hardy to -5°C (23°F). This plant is attractive and easy to grow. The Cape reed, (*Rhodocoma gigantea*) which has a much more lush effect like a soft bamboo, will reach 2.5m (8¼ft) and is likely to be just as hardy. The thatching reed, *Chondropetalum tectorum*, is by comparison a dumpy little plant at only 1.2m (4ft) tall with spiky grass-like foliage. In cooler climates, the latter is best grown in a pot and taken under cover in winter. The plume rush (*Restio tetraphyllus*) resembles a miniature bamboo as it forms a dense clump of smooth, slender stems. The thin, bright green thread-like foliage is carried from about halfway up each stem.

Restios like to grow in well-drained, moisture-retentive soil, so add a mixture of compost and grit at planting time to give suitable conditions. Ideally they prefer an acid soil and an open sunny position. Mulch well in the winter and feed sparingly in summer with a slow-release fertilizer.

Above Restios such as *Elegia capensis* have a very distinct and delicate foliage but their hardiness is still untested.

2 | CULTIVATION TECHNIQUES

Right This frothy mass of *Eragrostis airoides* makes the perfect foil for the eruption of the bold canna stems and leaves.

Starting Out

One of the most endearing characteristics of grasses is their ease of culture. They are uncomplicated plants, undemanding in their requirements and virtually always rewarding. In fact, they will often thrive in 'difficult' soils if we choose the right types. Specifically, there are those that like damp conditions and those that thrive in a dry environment. Most grasses prefer a sunny aspect but some will thrive in shade.

BUYING GRASSES

Plants are available from many sources – traditional nurseries, garden centres, plant fairs and by mail order. You will find the widest selection in the spring and early summer months. Generally, smaller, younger plants will establish quicker and faster than older clumps and they will be cheaper to buy. Plants from mail-order nurseries may be supplied as small 'plugs' which will require further growing on before planting out. Bamboos are generally much more expensive than grasses and are usually available in large pots only.

A good plant will have bright foliage colour, and the compost should not look loose, as if it has been recently repotted. Equally, a large plant with a faded label and hard compost encrusted with mosses may have been in a

Below These superbly grown grasses show the range of colours available and diversity of this fascinating group of plants.

Left In a mixed border grasses provide a valuable presence along-side colourful plants such as agapanthus, fuchsia and penstemon.

be necessary, but it can only be used in the growing season when weeds are actively growing.

Plants usually grow best in a soil that has been loosened by cultivation so that roots can easily penetrate and quickly establish. Dig or fork over small areas, loosening the soil down to about 20cm (8in). The use of a rotary cultivator in larger areas can speed up a tedious job but take care not to use such a machine in wet conditions as the structure of the soil can be badly damaged.

Most grasses naturally grow in poor, impoverished soils so additions of organic matter should be modest. Bamboos need more by comparison. If soils are inclined to be sticky and wet, the addition of generous amounts of sharp sand or grit will improve the much-needed drainage. Some of the more vigorous grasses such as pampas grass (*Cortaderia selloana*) will benefit from the addition of organic matter at planting time. Rushes and sedges like a damper soil and so add garden compost or other organic matter to help retain soil moisture.

Bamboos are greedy plants and will respond well to the addition of generous quantities of compost or manure before planting. You can also use a slow-release fertilizer such as bonemeal, which is rich in phosphates. Whatever you use, add it when you plant, mixing it in well with the topsoil.

garden centre rather too long and should be avoided.

Most plants now come with a cultural label, which will give a good indication of the situations in which it will thrive. You should always avoid impulse buying of plants which are not suitable for your garden conditions.

SOIL PREPARATION

As with most new plants, you must prepare the soil carefully before planting grasses. The removal of annual and perennial weeds, especially weed grasses, is important as they can be very difficult to eradicate at a later stage. This can be done in advance in a number of ways. Persistent hoeing and removal of weeds over a season will generally eradicate them. Alternatively, you can cover the site with a heavy membrane, such as an old carpet, and leave it for several months. This is a labour-saving way of smothering them out. If you need to clear a site quickly, use a weedkiller containing glyphosate as it kills roots as well as top growth. Several applications may

SOURCES OF HUMUS

To remain healthy, soils need humus, sometimes called organic matter. This is produced by the breakdown of animal or plant waste. As well as adding nutrients to the soil, humus helps with aeration and water retention, and brings life to the soil and encourages beneficial organisms.

- Farmyard manure
- Garden compost
- Leafmould
- Recycled green waste*
- Spent mushroom compost

*This is produced by many local authorities and can usually be obtained cheaply, often at a recycling or household waste centre.

Planting Grasses

Plant grasses in spring or early autumn. During the winter the ground is usually too cold and grasses may stay wet for too long before establishing new roots. Mid-spring is probably best for grasses, when the soil is still moist but starting to warm up. Bamboos, however, seem to establish well when planted in the autumn.

Plant small plants with a trowel. You will need a spade to dig a large enough hole to accommodate the rootball of larger plants. Place the plant in the hole and backfill with soil, firming in with the fingers or by treading gently. Grasses should always be planted at the same depth as they were in their pots with the 'crown' at soil level. Never bury the growing points under the surface. Bamboos, however, do respond well to planting slightly deeper. This seems to protect the roots from drought and cold and stimulate dormant root buds to grow. Try to plant when the soil is moist, but neither wet nor too dry.

HOW TO PLANT

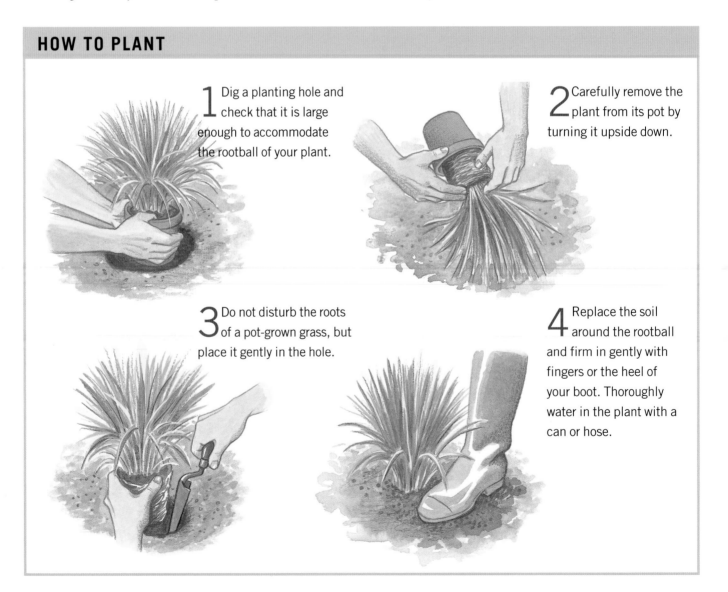

1 Dig a planting hole and check that it is large enough to accommodate the rootball of your plant.

2 Carefully remove the plant from its pot by turning it upside down.

3 Do not disturb the roots of a pot-grown grass, but place it gently in the hole.

4 Replace the soil around the rootball and firm in gently with fingers or the heel of your boot. Thoroughly water in the plant with a can or hose.

PLANT SPACING GUIDE

The small groundcover grasses such as blue fescue (*Festuca glauca*) can be planted about 30 cm (12 in) apart. (A)

The larger, mid-range grasses such as the Japanese silver grasses (*Miscanthus species*) should be planted 45–60cm (18–24in) apart. (B)

Big specimen grasses such as pampas (*Cortaderia selloana*) will need to be at least 1.2 m (4 ft) apart. (C)

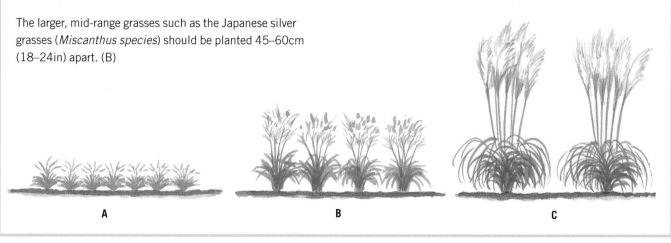

A   B   C

PLANT SPACING

With the immense variety of grasses available, it is almost impossible to give any precise directions with regard to spacing, although some general rules are possible. Taller, vigorous grasses will obviously require more space to grow than small compact ones. If the same plants are available in different-sized containers, it is generally better to plant more small plants closer together than fewer big plants at wider spacings. As we've already seen, small plants tend to establish and fill out more quickly than larger specimens. Unless you are planting a very small area, most plants, including grasses, look good in groups rather than as single plants. Try using groups of odd numbers – three, five or seven plants of one variety seem to look right.

As a rough guide, you should plant the small groundcover grasses, such as blue fescue (*Festuca glauca*) about 30cm (12in) apart. The larger grasses, such as the Japanese silver grasses (*Miscanthus*) and groundcover bamboos should be spaced 45-60cm (18-24in) apart. Big specimen grasses, such as pampas (*Cortaderia selloana*) and most bamboos will need to be at least 1.2m (4ft) apart to develop adequately.

When you are planning mixed plantings with other shrubs and herbaceous plants, you should try to estimate the eventual spread of all the plants. Another rule of thumb which often works is to space plants at half their ultimate height, but really it is not too important. If a bed is planted too sparsely, it is an easy matter to fill the gaps with later additions. An overplanted bed will quickly fill out, giving early interest, and can then be thinned by moving some plants to other areas. In fact, many skilled gardeners will reassess a planting scheme every year, moving plants, adding some and rejecting others completely. In this way a garden is always evolving and good planting schemes become outstanding ones!

Right Mixed borders should be thickly planted to give a profusion of foliage and flowers that seem to burst out of the ground.

Routine Care

As garden plants go, grasses need very little routine care and generally grow and thrive even when neglected. However, a little pampering won't go amiss and you will be rewarded with fresher foliage and abundant flowers. None of the techniques described here are demanding or expensive.

WATERING

Unless soil conditions are very wet, water in grasses immediately after planting to settle the soil around the roots. Newly planted grasses and bamboos will need regular watering in dry conditions during their first season to help them establish. Watering is best done with a sprinkler, which will give a gentle application – be sure to thoroughly moisten the soil each time. From the second season onwards, there should be no need to water unless the weather is particularly dry. Both grasses and bamboos roll their leaves when they are becoming dehydrated, so use this as an indication of the need to water.

MULCHING

Many grasses look good when displayed with a mulch of gravel. Gravel can simply be spread over the soil surface and, with time, it will naturally work into the ground improving the drainage. However, in time the surface effect will be lost as the gravel becomes incorporated.

It is perhaps better to first cover the soil with a mulching fabric so the gravel placed on top will remain on the surface. Lay the fabric over the prepared soil, then cut cross-shaped holes in it through which to plant. This gives a nice clean, dry surface to work on. A layer of gravel on top completes the scheme and hides the fabric.

MATERIALS FOR MULCHING
Gravel is the most familiar material used alongside grasses but others are possible.
- Bark chippings
- Cobbles
- Cocoa mulch
- Sea shells (washed)
- Tumbled glass mulch
- Wood chips

Left This grass garden at Knoll Gardens, Dorset, England, is mulched with gravel providing access and an effective weed barrier.

Sedges, rushes and bamboos are better mulched with an organic material such as leafmould or shredded bark which will help to maintain soil moisture as well as smother weeds. A mulch of 2.5cm (1in) should be adequate. While mulching, take care not to smother the crown of new plants. Indeed it may be preferable to plant a little shallow if you are planning to add a mulch. An organic mulch should be topped up annually.

Above The autumn foliage of the smoke bush makes a perfect background for the tawny seed heads of feather reed grass.

SEASONAL CARE

During the summer growing season, grasses generally require little attention. Weeding may be needed and the invasion of weed grasses, in particular, should be checked.

Troubleshooting

Apart from the odd pest or disease attack, the main problem you will encounter with ornamental grasses is caused by them being too healthy and vigorous. Keep the thugs in check by some timely cutting back, and make sure you tidy up all your grasses each year to keep them looking pristine.

PESTS AND DISEASES

Very few pests and diseases attack grasses. Powdery mildew may appear as white fungal patches on lower leaves, and rust will show as orange spots. You can treat both with an appropriate fungicide. Aphids (greenfly) occasionally attack and these can be controlled with a soft soap spray. In certain areas, mealy bugs may be a problem on Japanese silver grasses (*Miscanthus*). These appear as small cotton wool-like insects and are very difficult to control. You should cut out infected growths and destroy them by burning.

Whatever the disorder, it may be easier to cut infected foliage down to the ground and allow the plant to regrow rather than to spray. The new growth will usually quickly reclothe a plant in a good summer, although it may not mature enough to flower. Such a technique may be a valuable regular trick with some untidy grasses such as *Phalaris* which tend to become straggly by mid- summer.

Just occasionally in very damp conditions slugs and snails may attack grasses. They would not normally be favoured food material but it will depend what else is available. There are many proprietary slug controls on the market. For those that do not like the idea of pesticides there are organic controls.

CONTROLLING THUGS

A few grasses are so invasive that they can become problematic. This is usually because they spread by underground rhizomes or stolons. One such plant is lyme grass (*Leymus arenarius*), which spreads rampantly by rhizomes. In the right circumstances, such a habit can be beneficial and these plants can be used to great effect to colonize inhospitable soil or to stabilize loose soil banks. However, in a small garden they should be planted with great care.

Rampant colonizers can be restrained by enclosing them in a barrier such as a bottomless old bucket, sunk into the ground. Alternatively, you can grow them in a pot or container. If allowed to grow freely in the soil their advance can be checked by chopping back the clump during the growing season to sever the spreading growths. Such young peripheral shoots will usually be easy to remove without undue effort.

TIDYING UP

Once a year, most grasses need to be cut back. The dead growth from the previous season should be removed to ground level. Tidy-minded gardeners will want to do this in autumn to leave a pristine border over winter. This also has the benefit of removing seedheads before the seed is distributed, keeping prolific seeders in check.

Other gardeners, however, feel that grasses left untouched until spring have much to add to the winter garden. In this case cutting back should wait until early spring just before new growth starts. The dead foliage will also protect the crowns of any grasses that are on the borderline of hardiness.

Cut back the clumps almost to ground level using secateurs, shears or even a hedge trimmer. Evergreen grasses only need a light trim to remove the tips of burnt, winter-damaged leaves and old flower-heads. All the dead material should be raked off and taken away for composting, or chopped finely and left on site as a mulch. Traditionally, pampas grass has often been cleaned up by making a small bonfire in the middle of the clump to burn out the dry, dead material. Although you can do this, take great care not to kill the whole clump. In mild winters pampas remains evergreen and it may not be necessary to remove all the old foliage. Just selectively remove those leaves that have gone brown.

HOW TO CUT BACK

1 Start cutting back in late winter when grasses are beginning to look untidy.

2 Cut close to ground level using secateurs or shears, and avoiding any new growths.

3 Use a wire rake to gather up the rubbish and clean out loose material from the centre of the clump.

4 Loppers may be needed for a few plants, such as some of the stronger-growing *Miscanthus*.

5 If you have a lot of grasses, a hedge trimmer can be used to speed up the job.

PRACTICAL TIPS

• Clearing up the cut material can be a bit tedious. Before cutting, bundle the old stems together with string and then sever the whole clump near to the ground.

• Be aware that some grasses such as pampas have sharp edges to their leaves and vicious teeth. Strong garden gloves should be used when working with grasses.

Growing Bamboos

Bamboos are often moodily evocative of faintly remembered holidays, romantic gardens visited or childhood 'jungle' explorations. As well as adding texture, structure and colour to a garden, bamboos add sound and movement. Once described as 'grasses with attitude', bamboos are architectural plants with a strong vertical emphasis.

Although they are members of the grass family, bamboos are so distinct as to warrant a space on their own in this book. Bamboos are simply woody grasses with a permanent framework and often grow to several metres in height. Bamboo has always been a very important material in Far Eastern cultures and is used for many purposes. Although modern materials may have replaced its use in some areas, it is still valued for making many everyday items – the strong canes can be used for house and bridge building and the foliage for thatching. Stem sections can be made into buckets, saucepans and cups. Because they are hollow, bamboo stems can also be made into pipes and even musical instruments. The young shoots of certain bamboos are eaten as a vegetable, a wine is made from them in some areas, and an all-

purpose medicinal elixir has been made and revered for thousands of years.

Bamboos occur in the wild on all continents except Europe. However, as there are many hardy as well as tropical species, they can now be found growing throughout the world. Botanically, bamboos are a complex group of plants. Because they flower so rarely, the opportunity to examine them in detail seldom occurs and their study is incomplete. Botanists do not agree on the naming of many bamboos and have often changed their names in the past. This leads to considerable confusion for the gardener.

CULMS AND COLOURS

It is often the canes, correctly known as culms, which are the main feature of bamboos. They come in a variety of colours – green, gold, rich brown, murky black and purplish. Some are thin, others fat, and may even be striped. Others are knobbly or have a zigzag form, such as *Phyllostachys aureosulcata alata*, not a plant for a tidy person! Bamboo leaves are all quite similar but vary in size from finger-slender to chunky and broad, with colours from minty green through to those with gold and silver variegations.

Bamboos range in size from giants reaching over 20m (65½ft) tall, down to dwarf species growing no more than 30cm (12in). Between those extremes there is a multitude of different types suitable for almost any garden situation. Although many bamboos may be hardy enough to grow in temperate climates, they may not achieve their full potential and the culms will be shorter and thinner than those on plants grown in warmer climates. Some of

Left The vivid golden stems of *Phyllostachys vivax* 'Aureocaulis' make it a highly desirable garden plant.

the taller types have a tree-like presence and can be used as specimen plants on their own. Many are dense enough to act as screens or hedges and have the advantage of needing minimal trimming. Other dwarf types are thick enough to be used as groundcover.

HOW THEY GROW

Bamboos are evergreen plants. The new culms come from underground stems called rhizomes. The culms are divided into sections by the distinct nodes. In most bamboos, the sections between the nodes is hollow. The growth of new culms is very fast, particularly in tropical species and in good seasons. When they reach their ultimate height, they will make no further growth but will survive for 5–10 years at that height.

The leaves are borne on small branches from the main

Above The vigorous growth of this brightly coloured *Phyllostachys aurea* is restrained within a bed of sleepers.

culm. The foliage consists of sheaths which encircle the culm as well as true leaves. The sheaths often become papery and brown and remain attached to the plant long after they are dead.

While grasses generally prefer poor soil, bamboos perform best in a rich, moist soil. When preparing the soil for planting bamboos, it is important to incorporate generous amounts of compost or manure to enrich the soil. Being shallow rooted, they respond well to a good thick mulch of bark, compost or leafmould. It is worth treating them well as, once established, successive generations of culms will be thicker and taller than the previous generations.

Bamboo Features

Bamboos have many attractive qualities which make them valuable garden plants.
They are suitable for a whole range of uses, from groundcover and border fillers to
towering specimen plants and thick rustling screens. With a little imagination,
these plants can be spectacular.

FLOWERING

Bamboos only come into flower very occasionally
rather than every year. Their flowers are small and
inconspicuous. Sometimes the entire plant flowers and
then most of the leaves are dropped and the plant lives
off its food reserves. After seed production, the plant
may die completely, which can be very disappointing
for the gardener.

Strangely, it is not unusual for many plants of the
same type, growing in far distant places, to all flower in
the same year and then die. One hypothesis is that as
bamboos are propagated by division, these are all parts of
the same original parent plant and they therefore all
mature, flower and seed at the same time. It should be
emphasized that bamboos flower very rarely and do not
always die afterwards, so this should not deter you from
trying them.

SCREENS AND SPECIMEN PLANTS

Bamboos make excellent screens. Choose a species that
will grow to the desired height without any need for
trimming, although this can be done if required. In fact
regular pruning of both the top and the sides of the plants
will result in thicker more dense growth. Such pruning
should always be done with secateurs.

Below Bamboo has been used as a building material for centuries
and these giant bamboo poles make an innovative retaining wall.

One of the best and toughest bamboos for a screen is *Pseudosasa japonica* which grows to about 2m (6½ft). The delicate-looking *Fargesia nitida* grows to a similar height. On a grander scale there is *Semiarundinaria fastuosa* which, under ideal conditions, can achieve 5m (16½ft).

Bamboos can be very useful as specimens in a garden. They usually reach their ultimate height quite quickly, only gaining slowly in the size of the clump. Species such as *Chusquea culeou* or *Fargesia murieliae* are not invasive and remain as a tight clump. Even the more invasive types can be used as specimens in a lawn as mowing will deter invading new shoots.

ORIENTAL SCHEMES

The most traditional use of bamboo is in an Oriental-style garden. Such designs are usually quite minimal, with raked gravel or sand, groupings of boulders and water features. Other specimen plants such as dwarf maple (*Acer palmatum*), irises, azaleas, wisteria and pine trees may be used as well. Genuine Japanese gardens are quite complex with a great depth of meaning and mystique but this should not stop you from trying to create an Oriental-style garden of your own using bamboos. You can even use them for bonsai culture; *Phyllostachys humilis* is regularly used in Japan.

GROUNDCOVER

There are several dwarf bamboos which excel as groundcover plants. When used in the right situation, we can exploit their invasiveness to create a dense carpet of weed-smothering foliage. *Pleioblastus pygmaeus*, *P. auricomus* and *P. variegata* all make excellent groundcover plants, growing to no more than 1m (3ft). Among them there are green, gold and white variegations. As with all groundcover plantings, make sure the soil is free of perennial weeds before planting.

CONTAINERS

Bamboos make excellent plants for pots and other containers. Black bamboo (*Phyllostachys nigra*) or *Phyllostachys vivax* 'Aureocaulis' would make a good specimen in a large container. Plant them in a good soil-based potting compost and take care never to allow them to dry out. Feed regularly during the late spring and summer months.

Above Burnished steel containers and an orange background make the perfect setting for this black bamboo (*Phyllostachys nigra*).

Depending on their rate of growth, container-grown bamboos will need repotting after two or three years. You can move the plant on to a larger container or to a permanent site in the ground. If you want to keep the plant in the same container, reduce the size of the rootball by dividing the plant or just carefully removing some of the root system and outer portions of the plant to make room for new potting compost. This should regenerate the plant for a further few years. The root systems of bamboos can be very strong so take care that older plants do not split valuable pots. In this situation it may be better to grow the bamboo in a plastic pot and plunge into the treasured pot.

Bamboo Care

As woody members of the grass family, bamboos do have some particular cultural requirements, however the same principles apply to buying and planting bamboos as grasses (see pages 18–21). Nevertheless once again, they are generally easy plants to grow and rewarding for new and experienced gardeners.

PRUNING

Established clumps of bamboo will benefit from annual pruning to thin out the older, dead or weak culms. This improves the general appearance of the clump and encourages the growth of new culms. Do this in the spring using sharp secateurs or loppers.

You could also remove some of the lower side shoots to expose the culms and make the clump more attractive. This should be done in late summer or early autumn. This treatment is particularly effective with bamboos with colourful culms.

ROUTINE CARE

Established bamboos need little other care, although an annual mulch and feed in the spring will encourage strong new growth. Any good organic matter such as garden

MULCHING
Shovel mulch around the bamboo plants and spread it out with a rake.

compost, farmyard manure, leafmould, bark chippings or spent mushroom compost can be used. You can feed with any general-purpose balanced, granular fertilizer, although the modern slow-release types are best.

In the summer, water bamboos during dry spells to keep them in peak condition. Remember that it is essential to thoroughly wet the soil, preferably with a sprinkler, so that the water penetrates to the roots.

For a neat and tidy finish, cut the dwarf groundcover types of *Pleioblastus* to the ground each year and they will readily regenerate.

If grown outside, bamboos do not usually suffer from pests and diseases. If they are grown in a greenhouse, they may be attacked by whitefly or red spider mite. Rabbits or squirrels can be attracted to the young shoots of the chunkier bamboos. All bamboos are resistant to honey fungus (*Armillaria*) so they will happily grow in ground where there are old tree stumps that may be infected.

INVASIVENESS

Bamboos have the unjust reputation of being invasive, impossible to eradicate and generally nuisance plants. There are a few that will take over the garden if given a chance but these are the minority. If you are concerned, avoid *Chimonobambusa, Phyllostachys violescens, Pleioblastus*

CUTTING BACK

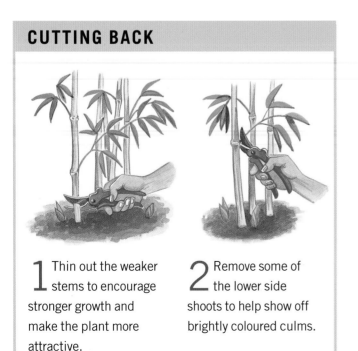

1 Thin out the weaker stems to encourage stronger growth and make the plant more attractive.

2 Remove some of the lower side shoots to help show off brightly coloured culms.

and *Sasa*. Choose clump-forming types rather than those with runners unless you want an area colonized – even invasive plants have their value in the right place.

If you must grow these species, you can try planting them within a barrier. This must be something substantial like a large metal container or even a section of concrete drain. Plastic is possible but it may not be substantial enough to withstand the onslaughts of a determined bamboo!

CONTROLLING BY TRIMMING

Possibly an easier way of controlling invasive bamboos is to trim the roots annually. This can be done in any season, but winter is probably the best time. Dig a small trench about 30cm (12in) deep all around the perimeter of the clump of canes. All the exposed rhizomes should be cut with the spade or with secateurs. Follow the cut end into the surrounding soil and remove it. The trench can be refilled with soil or, ideally, loose compost which will feed the plant and make next year's job that much easier.

If bamboos have become a problem and need removing, use a herbicide. If you want to reuse the area, you will have to dig out the clump. After digging out most of the roots, the area should be left fallow and the regrowth treated with glyphosate during the summer months. This will kill the entire plant. Several treatments may be needed.

LIMITING SPREAD
Sink a large pot into the ground before planting an invasive bamboo.

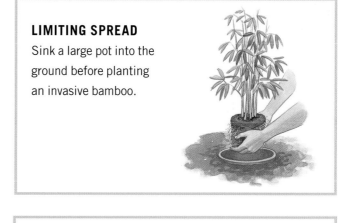

RUNNERS AND CLUMPERS
Bamboos with running rhizomes travel some distance before making new culms. (A)

Clumping bamboos still have rhizomes but they turn up and develop new culms without extending. (B)

A

B

TRIMMING THE ROOTS

1 Sharpen a spade especially for this using a whetstone.

2 Dig a shallow trench around the main plant about 30cm (12in) away.

3 Cut through all the spreading rhizomes with the spade or secateurs.

4 Tease the cut sections of rhizomes from the soil outside the trench. Refill the trench with soil or compost.

3 | PROPAGATION

Right The rather profligate seeding habit of Bowle's golden grass
can be seen as a virtue when mixed with a blue viola such as this.

Propagating Grasses

Both grasses and bamboos are most commonly propagated by dividing the clumps to make a number of new plants. Grasses can also be grown from seed and a few can be raised from cuttings. The techniques for grasses and bamboos are, however, somewhat different so they will be described separately. (See page 38.)

DIVISION

Most of the grasses that you will want to propagate will be named cultivars, the artificially bred varieties. These can only be propagated by division as they will not come true from seed. Division is also essential when old clumps become congested and start to lose their vigour. This usually happens every three or four years.

The best time to divide grasses is in late spring when the soil is warming up but is still moist. However, some of the tougher types can be done in the autumn.

Dig up an existing clump with a fork or spade. I find that it is best to use a fork as it retains most of the roots that can then be shaken loose of soil. With smaller grasses, you should be able to tease the clump apart by hand into smaller usable portions. With larger ones, you will need to use two garden forks placed back to back to lever the clumps apart. Unless the clump is very small, aim to break it into three or more small plants with roots.

TOUGH CLUMPS

You may need to dig up big tough clumps with a spade, then chop up the rootball with a spade, axe or saw. Such treatment is obviously not ideal as roots will be damaged in the process. However, the grasses that will require such rough treatment will typically be robust enough to survive despite it.

If the clump is old, the centre may be weak or dead, so discard the central portion and use the more vigorous outer sections. If the divisions have lush top growth, reduce the leaves somewhat to prevent excess loss of moisture, and trim any lengthy roots.

DIVIDING SMALL CLUMPS

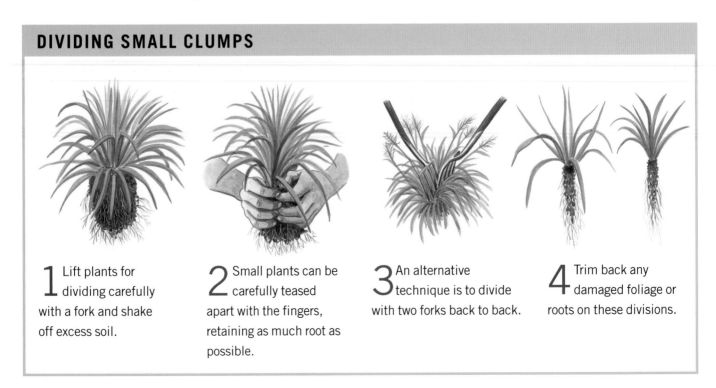

1 Lift plants for dividing carefully with a fork and shake off excess soil.

2 Small plants can be carefully teased apart with the fingers, retaining as much root as possible.

3 An alternative technique is to divide with two forks back to back.

4 Trim back any damaged foliage or roots on these divisions.

DIVIDING LARGE CLUMPS

1 Big clumps may be very heavy and need digging up with a spade.

2 Chop up the clump with an old saw kept for this purpose.

3 Alternatively, an axe can be very effective but handle with care.

REPLANTING DIVISIONS

Divisions should be planted back into freshly prepared soil as soon as possible without letting any part of the plant dry out. Water in well and keep the soil moist until the divisions are growing vigorously again. If you don't have a border ready, heel them into a spare patch of soil or pot them up to avoid them deteriorating.

In some cases it may be useful to pot up divisions and grow them on for a while until they are large enough to be planted out. Choose a suitable sized pot for the divisions and use any good well-drained potting compost. Don't forget, if you are dividing a number of named grasses, to renew labels or write fresh name tags for potted divisions.

GROWING FROM RUNNERS

Some grasses, such as gardener's garters (*Phalaris arundinacea*), produce runners. These are small shoots that appear a short distance from the main plant. You can easily detach these and use as divisions without disturbing the main plant.

CUTTINGS

The giant reed (*Arundo donax*) is a handsome woody grass with stems like a bamboo. This plant can be propagated by cuttings in early autumn. Cut stem sections about 30cm (12in) long, remove the leaves and lay the stems in a shallow tray of water. Keep the tray in a warm environment such as a propagator.

Small side shoots will develop from the nodes, and then eventually roots. These can be detached, carefully transferred to small pots of compost and grown on in a frost-free greenhouse ready for planting out the following summer.

TAKING CUTTINGS

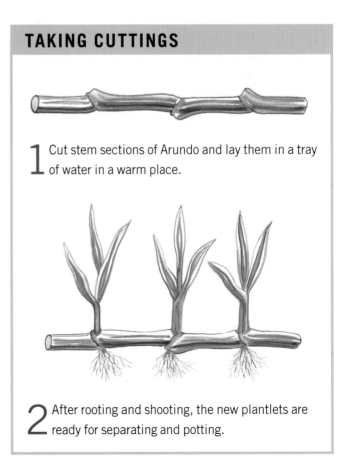

1 Cut stem sections of Arundo and lay them in a tray of water in a warm place.

2 After rooting and shooting, the new plantlets are ready for separating and potting.

Growing From Seed

Grasses readily grow from seed but remember that very few will breed true. Grasses are wind pollinated so crosses may have taken place with other grasses quite some distance away. You can sow seed from your own grasses and obtain interesting results, but don't assume that they will be the same as the parent plant. Sow seed in mid-spring.

Although seed can be sown directly outside, the best results will be from seed sown in a cool greenhouse. Sow in pots in a proprietary seed compost, cover the seed lightly with sieved compost, and then cover the pots with polythene. Keep at about 16°C (61°F) and uncover the pots as soon as any seedlings appear.

When the seedlings are big enough to handle, prick them out into small pots or seed trays containing potting or multipurpose compost. Prick the seedlings out in clumps of three to five so that you get decent sized plants quite quickly. Grow on in a cool greenhouse in a well-lit situation.

SOWING GRASS SEEDS

1 Sow grass seeds thinly in pots of moist seed compost.

2 Cover the seed with a thin layer of sieved compost and label.

3 These young grass seedlings are ready for pricking out.

4 ◁ Prick out the seedlings in clumps of three to five, taking care not to damage the roots.

5 ▷ Pot on the clumps into individual pots or well-spaced in seed trays in a multipurpose or potting compost.

SOWING ANNUAL GRASSES

All annual grasses have to be grown from seed each year. They are often sown directly into a prepared seedbed outside in mid-spring. Keeping the grasses weed free later on is easier if you sow the seed in drills about 15cm (6in) apart.

Annual grasses can also be sown in pots grown under glass and planted out like bedding plants when they reach a suitable size. Half-hardy types, such as the ornamental forms of maize and the new purple millet (*Pennisetum glaucum* 'Purple Majesty'), must be done this way to protect them from frost. You should only plant them outside when all danger of frost is passed.

ANNUAL GRASSES

All annual plants complete their life cycles within a single season. So it is not surprising that annual grasses flower prolifically as they race on to set seed and guarantee their existence for the next year. Annual grasses are not so widely grown as perennials yet they are surprisingly easy. As well as providing excellent garden displays, they are also first-rate for drying.

Annual grasses can be used anywhere that you might want to use perennial grasses but it is probably among temporary summer displays that they are most commonly

SOWING IN DRILLS

If you sow annual grass seed in shallow drills, it will be easier to remove weeds when they appear by hoeing between the rows of germinating grasses.

seen. Most can be raised easily in a cool greenhouse and associate well with summer bedding. A few plants can be useful fillers where there are gaps in a border.

The foliage of most annual grasses is unpretentious, although there are a few with interesting leaves. In particular the variegated maize (*Zea mays* 'Gigantea Quadricolor') is quite spectacular. It grows tall with pink and white variegations and is often used as a dot plant in summer bedding or as part of a subtropical display. There are also versions of maize which have coloured cobs and these can be dried for interesting floral displays in the winter. The newly introduced purple millet (*Pennisetum glaucum* 'Purple Majesty') is a spectacular foliage plant with rich purple leaves. These plants are half-hardy so need to be raised in a cool greenhouse and not planted out until all danger of frost is passed.

The quaking grasses *Briza maxima* and *B. minima* are appealing little plants which yield copious quantities of locket shaped flower-heads with a touch of red. The flowers of rabbit-tail grass (*Lagurus ovatus*) are more like small pointed tufts or paintbrushes in a soft green.

The somewhat taller foxtail barley (*Hordeum jubatum*) has long barley-shaped heads with silky hairs called awns. As they mature they turn from green to pink and eventually brown.

Left Foxtail barley (*Hordeum jubatum*) must be grown from seed each year as it is an annual.

Propagating Bamboos

Bamboos are most readily propagated by division, a process which is easy to undertake and requires no specialist equipment. Although this can be done at almost any time of the year, the best time is early spring. In areas with mild winters, autumn is also a good time. Spare plants always make great gifts.

On any clump of bamboo there will usually be some groups of culms around the edge and it is these you want to remove. A good division will have about three young culms and be a small distance from the main plant.

Gently excavate around the new division and expose the roots and rhizomes, taking care to avoid damaging them. When the structure is clear, sever the rhizome connecting the division to the main plant using a sharp spade or loppers. Lift the division with as much soil and undisturbed roots as possible. The division can then be replanted in fresh soil or potted up to grow on for later planting.

If the division has a large root system, this should balance the top growth which can be left intact. With tall bamboos and divisions with a small root system, prune back the culms to prevent excess loss of moisture and wind rock.

LARGE CLUMPS AND POTTED BAMBOOS

Dividing large old clumps to create divisions is possible, but the root system will be very resilient and you will need a sharpened spade or axe to cut through the tough mass of intermingled rhizomes.

Dividing potted bamboos may also be difficult where there is a tight mass of rhizomes. After removing the plant from the pot, it can be helpful to wash off the excess soil with a hose so you can see what you've got. The plant can then usually be divided with sharp secateurs or an old saw. Larger divisions often take better than small ones which may die. Although not essential, a cold greenhouse or polythene tunnel can be useful to house potted divisions. It should be kept cool and lightly shaded. The damp atmosphere and gentle extra warmth will help the new divisions establish and grow away without too much leaf stress.

BAMBOO DIVISIONS

A good bamboo division will have several stems, each with some vigorous roots. If the stems are very tall, or the roots very small, trim the culms down to prevent excess moisture loss.

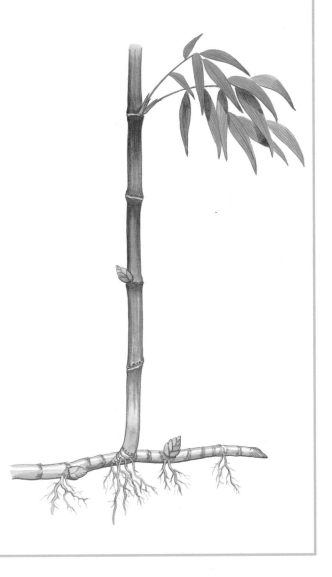

RHIZOME SECTIONS

Remove sections of rhizome from the parent plant, each with at least one bud. Trim off any damaged sections of rhizome before potting up. Place in a coldframe or cold greenhouse to grow on. Water sparingly until new roots and shoots are apparent.

Above Although it only spreads slowly, *Pleioblastus shibuyanus* 'Tsubio' can be propagated from small rhizome sections.

PROPAGATING FROM RHIZOMES

Some bamboos, such as *Pleioblastus*, *Sasa* and *Fargesia*, have freely running rhizomes. These plants can be propagated by removing sections of rhizome with buds. This is best done in early spring. Cut the rhizomes into small sections each with at least one bud. Pot up the sections and place in a coldframe or cool greenhouse. Growth should occur in six to eight weeks. This is a slower method of propagation than division, but may be useful for producing larger quantities of plants. This technique is particularly useful for propagating the groundcover bamboos such as *Pleioblastus*, as a larger quantity of smaller plants will be valuable for colonising a new area quickly and evenly. Such divisions will probably be ready for planting out a year after propagation.

4 | GRASSES AND BAMBOOS IN THE GARDEN

Right The rounded tufts of this blue fescue (*Festuca glauca*) echo the shapes of these white cobbles creating a satisfying harmony.

General Tips

Planting grasses or bamboos alone, whether in broad sweeps of one species or in a mixed grouping, can be stunning and gives an almost dream-like ethereal effect. However, the most spectacular results are usually achieved when they are used in plantings with other contrasting plants.

USING THESE PROJECTS

The following projects are suggestions of different ways of combining grasses with other exciting plants and various situations in which grasses can be effectively used. The schemes are not intended to be definitive but to be freely interpreted according to the site available, weather conditions etc.

For example, no attempt has been made to give a scale for these projects and numbers of plants are only loosely indicated in the plans. In general, garden plants seem to look right in odd-numbered groups; threes, fives, sevens and so on. For very small gardens, the schemes could be created with groups of threes or even single plants of larger species. Likewise in larger plots the groups can be much bigger and may be repeated, creating a rhythm through the border. Equally, some gardeners may wish to use an idea in an irregular island bed, whereas others may wish to take the same scheme and plant a formal border. Inevitably, in this book grasses dominate the schemes. As such, the size of the grass groups should be larger than the supporting plants, although the proportions of this will be a matter of personal taste.

I hope that you will be inspired by the themes proposed and add other suitable plants of your own choosing. Garden centres and nurseries have an amazing wealth of plants available and there will be many others that will fit all the schemes.

CONTRASTING COMPANIONS

Plants with particularly large or bold leaves generally make the best contrast with grasses. The familiar elephant's ears (*Bergenia*) is a sound example. The leaves of bergenia are broad and horizontal compared to the narrow vertical foliage of grasses. Grasses are generally taller than the bergenia, so the grass can either be positioned behind the bergenia, or in front so that the bergenia is seen through the veil of the grass foliage. This idea works just as well with hostas.

Many other plants will provide a similar contrast:
- *Acanthus spinosus*
- *Crambe cordifolia*
- *Fatsia japonica*
- *Hedera colchica*
- *Hosta sieboldiana*
- *Vitis coignetiae*

Above The broad leaves and bold flowers of the hosta are a robust contrast to the thread-like foliage and delicate flowers of the grasses.

PERFECT PARTNERS

Bergenias are easy to grow and are the perfect planting companions for grasses of all types. Tall grasses can make a fine contrast when planted behind the fleshy leaves of bergenia, accentuating their vertical aspect. (A)

When the grass is planted in the front, the bergenias are visible through the soft veil of grass stems. (B)

A   B

OTHER GRASS-LIKE PLANTS

There are a few plants that, although they are not actually grasses, have a similar appearance and make good companions in a mixed planting. One of the best is *Ophiopogon planiscapus* 'Nigrescens' which has probably the blackest foliage available. It is slow growing, with narrow strap-like foliage about 15cm (6in) tall. It looks startling amongst gold foliage, white flowers or when growing between snowy white cobbles. This plant takes quite a while to achieve a dense clump, so it is worth planting several small plants together.

The foliage and growth habit of various different types of *Liriope* is very similar but the leaves are either green or variegated. These plants are tolerant of sun or shade and are often used as groundcover. There are various handsome yellow and white variegated forms, such as 'John Burch'. The long-lasting flowers are mauve, lilac or white in dense spikes very much like grape hyacinths.

Plants in the genus *Acorus* are grass-like in appearance and some have a name that indicates this, such as the Japanese rush (*Acorus gramineus*) which is usually seen in the brilliantly variegated form 'Ogon'. Like its close relative *Acorus calamus*, it is best grown in a damp situation.

Tulbaghia is a small genus of plants within the onion family, all of which have narrow grass-like foliage. The most common is *Tulbaghia violacea* which grows to about 45cm (18in) high. It is a perverse plant because the foliage has a strong, pungent onion smell, while the delicate violet flowers have a sweet perfume. The trick is to smell it without touching it! There is a variegated form called 'Silver Lace'. Although charming, both are tender and a bit tricky to grow. Try them in a patio pot and bring under cover over winter.

Above Liriopes make excellent long-lasting evergreen groundcover plants, with the bonus of flowers as well as attractive foliage.

Prairie Planting

This is a fairly new style of gardening that draws inspiration from the North American prairies or steppe landscapes with their open grasslands interspersed with broadleaf flowering species. This approach has been particularly developed in Europe by designers such as Piet Oudolf. Although many prairie gardens are on a large scale, there are also many very successful ones in small gardens.

There are finer points and some differences between the European and the North American interpretation of prairie planting. Oudolf emphasizes that shapes are more important than the flowers themselves. His schemes have bold groups of giant angelicas (*Angelica gigas*), huge eupatoriums and tall thalictrums. Great swirls of grasses such as *Molinia caerulea*, *Deschampsia cespitosa*, *Panicum virgatum* and *Miscanthus sinensis* will link together the big groups. A scheme that mimicked a genuine steppe environment would have a simpler, sweeping landscape with hovering yellow daisies and stands of simple grasses. There would be no attempt at a colour scheme.

WHAT IS PRAIRIE PLANTING?

In essence it is a naturalistic style that uses ornamental grasses together with strong growing cultivars of herbaceous plants to produce a very soft, soothing effect with gentle waves of natural colour. In some ways it is a cross between a herbaceous border and a flowering meadow. Just like a meadow planting, it is designed to be walked through and prairie plantings may fill the whole space with pathways running through so that the effect can be experienced at close quarters. These types of landscape are often most successful when established on nutrient poor soil in an open sunny site. After planting, mulch the surface of the soil with bark or gravel.

Above A good prairie planting will be a billowing mass of grasses interspersed with colour like these golden-headed achilleas.

GRASSES FOR PRAIRIE PLANTING

- *Cortaderia selloana*
- *Deschampsia cespitosa*
- *Helictotrichon sempervirens*
- *Miscanthus sinensis* 'Kleine Fontäne'
- *Miscanthus sinensis* 'Malepartus'
- *Panicum virgatum*
- *Pennisetum alopecuroides* 'Hameln'

HERBACEOUS PERENNIALS FOR PRAIRIE PLANTING

- *Achillea* 'Summerwine'
- *Angelica gigas*
- *Echinacea purpurea* 'White Swan'
- *Eupatorium purpureum*
- *Helenium* 'Moorheim Beauty'
- *Monarda* 'Ruby Glow'
- *Persicaria amplexicaulis* 'Atrosanguinea'
- *Rudbeckia* 'Goldsturm'
- *Thalictrum aquilegiifolium*
- *Verbena bonariensis*

PRAIRIE PLANTING PROJECT

This example shows a reduced colour palette of deep wine, lavender tints and rich yellows, all tied together with various shades of green. The ruby reds come from the giant angelica (*Angelica gigas*), Achillea 'Summerwine' and the *Eupatorium purpureum*. The contrasting rich golds are provided by *Helenium* 'Moorheim Beauty' and cone flowers (*Rudbeckia* 'Goldsturm'). The long flowering Michaelmas daisy (*Aster* x *frikartii* 'Mönch') and threads of

Verbena bonariensis give the cooler tints. Sweeps of tufted hair grass (*Deschampsia cespitosa*) and panic grass (*Panicum virgatum*) are punctuated by taller stands of golden oats (*Stipa gigantea*). As well as the medley of colours, there are differing heights from the compact dumpy michaelmas daisy, through to the soaring angelica. Differing heights, colours and shapes all add up to a display with infinite interest that can be

enjoyed at close proximity from the winding path that bisects the scheme.

One way of creating a prairie landscape is by sowing a seed mix. These are specialist seed mixes containing herbaceous perennials and ornamental grasses. Before sowing it is essential to clear the soil of all perennial weeds (see page 19). Weeding may be needed in the early months to encourage establishment of the desired species.

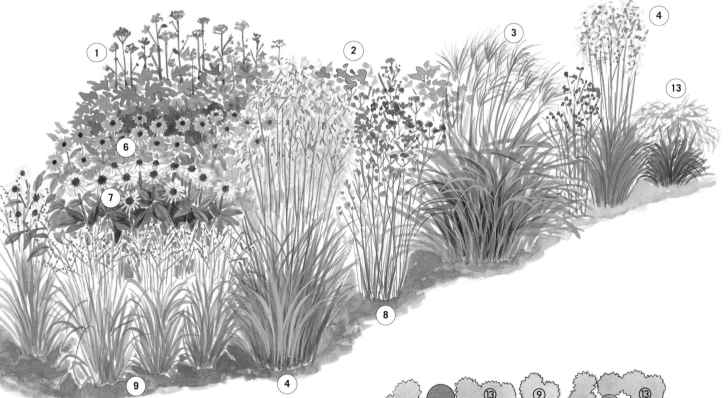

KEY TO PLANTING PLAN AND ELEVATION

1 *Angelica gigas*
2 *Thalictrum aquilegiifolium*
3 *Miscanthus sinensis* 'Silberfeder'
4 *Stipa gigantea*
5 *Aster x frikartii* 'Mönch'
6 *Rudbeckia* 'Goldsturm'
7 *Echinacea purpurea* 'White Swan'
8 *Verbena bonariensis*
9 *Panicum virgatum*
10 *Achillea* 'Summerwine'
11 *Helenium* 'Moorheim Beauty'
12 *Eupatorium purpureum*
13 *Deschampsia cespitosa*

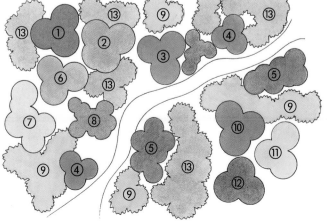

The Urban Jungle

About a hundred years ago, a garden style called "sub-tropical" was *de rigeur*. Fashions come around again and once more it is very fashionable to create exotic plantings. Many grasses and bamboos fit in with this style. Exotic gardening places emphasis on foliage, particularly plants with large or unusual leaves and architectural shapes. Grasses provide their own contribution as well as contrasting with those plants with larger, broader leaves.

The general speed of growth is also just right for the exotic garden where the purpose is to create a jungle-like atmosphere as quickly as possible. Many of the other subjects used will be strong growers and grasses and bamboos will compete well. Even if some of the grasses do spread, it may well enhance the lush, atmosphere!

Most good exotic gardens employ a background of hardy shrubs and herbaceous plants, which are complemented by tender species planted each season. Bamboos are part of the permanent framework but grasses can be either permanent or planted annually. As some of the species in this scheme are of borderline hardiness, the chosen site should be well sheltered, particularly in temperate climates. Good drainage and well prepared soil with plenty of compost are the ideal conditions in which to encourage vigorous growth.

Above Close planted bamboos and other exotics can create a shady green oasis that is totally hardy and very low maintenance.

BAMBOOS FOR EXOTIC BORDERS
- *Fargesia nitida*
- *Phyllostachys bambusoides* 'Castillonis'
- *Pleioblastus auricomus*
- *Pseodosasa japonica*

HARDY EXOTIC SHRUBS
- *Aralia elata*
- *Fatsia japonica*
- *Musa basjoo*
- *Trachycarpus fortunei*

GRASSES FOR EXOTIC PLANTINGS
- *Arundo donax* 'Variegata'
- *Cortaderia selloana* 'Gold Band'
- *Elegia capensis*
- *Miscanthus sinensis* 'Cosmopolitan'
- *Molinea caerulea* 'Variegata'
- *Pennisetum glaucum* 'Purple Majesty'
- *Pennisetum setaceum* 'Rubrum'
- *Phalaris arundinaceae* 'Feesey'

TENDER EXOTICS
- *Canna* 'Durban'
- *Coleus* 'Pineapple Beauty'
- *Dahlia* 'Bishop of Llandaff'
- *Ricinus communis* 'Impala'

URBAN JUNGLE PLANTING PROJECT

The hardy species such as the bamboos, Japanese angelica tree (*Aralia eleta*) and palm (*Trachycarpus fortunei*), can be planted during the winter or spring months. These plants are likely to remain permanently and will provide shelter for the seasonal plantings. The banana (*Musa basjoo*) should not be planted until late spring but can remain permanently in position if its 'trunk' is wrapped each winter. Most of the grasses can be planted in late spring. The tender plants, including the variegated maize (*Zea mays* 'Gigantea Quadricolor') should be added after all danger of frost is passed in early summer. A scheme such as this should be watered well in dry spells and fed regularly to create the lush, jungle-like atmosphere.

A variation on the exotic style is the 'cool lush' effect where we can use a lot of foliage plants, mainly in green, avoiding brightly coloured flowers or variegated foliage. Bamboo works exceptionally well in this situation and I know of a wonderful small jungle-like garden which is comprised of mainly bamboo with a small bark-strewn clearing in the centre.

KEY TO PLANTING PLAN AND ELEVATION

1 *Pseudosasa japonica*
2 *Canna* 'Durban'
3 *Fargesia nitida*
4 *Trachycarpus fortunei*
5 *Phyllostachys bambusoides* 'Castillonis'
6 *Ricinus communis* 'Impala'
7 *Zea mays* 'Gigantea Quadricolor'
8 *Cortaderia selloana* 'Gold band'
9 *Aralia elata*
10 *Pleioblastus auricomus*
11 *Musa basjoo*
12 *Arundo donax* 'Variegata'
13 *Elegia capensis*
14 *Phalaris arundinaceae* 'Feesey'
15 *Coleus* 'Pineapple Beauty'
16 *Molinea caerulea* 'Variegata'
17 *Pennisetum setaceum* 'Rubrum'

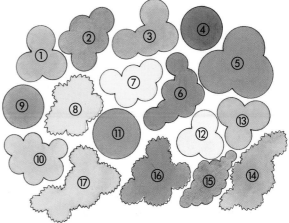

Hot and Dry

Many gardeners have seen the effects of global warming as distinct changes in climate, with many areas experiencing extremes of wet as well as hot, dry periods. Some gardeners rise to the challenge by experimenting with new plants and styles, particularly trying out plantings that thrive in dry situations. This also makes sense from an ecological point of view as a way to conserve water.

With careful choice of plants, hot and dry gardens can still have a rich colourful display throughout the year. Inevitably many grasses fit into this category. A dry garden can make use of just grasses, or a mixture of grasses with other plants. As most of the plants that are suitable for growing in these conditions need to be dry, it is essential to prepare the soil so that they will remain well drained throughout the year. If you have a loose sandy soil or minimal rainfall, you will need to choose dry garden plants anyway.

Many grasses actively thrive in dry situations. Other varieties that prefer moister conditions but tend to be invasive will grow more slowly in a dry regime and are less likely to be troublesome.

DRY GARDEN STYLE
Dry gardens all have a certain similarity, but with a little ingenuity you can create a specific style. Desert-style gardens have very sparse planting, with outcrops of rock and succulent plants such as yucca or prickly pear (*Opuntia*). Mediterranean dry gardens are more closely planted but have a very specific mix of plants. As well as grasses, Mediterranean gardens use lavender, rosemary, sage, thyme and upright conifers. Such plantings will have year round interest.

Left Many grasses such as Spanish oat grass, (*Stipa gigantea*) revel in hot, dry conditions and need no watering.

DRY GARDEN GRASSES
- *Carex comans* 'Frosted Curls'
- *Festuca glauca* 'Elijah Blue'
- *Helictotrichon sempervirens*
- *Koeleria glauca*
- *Leymus arenarius*
- *Panicum virgatum* 'Heavy Metal'
- *Pennisetum villosum*
- *Stipa gigantea*
- *Stipa tenuissima*

OTHER PLANTS FOR THE DRY GARDEN
- *Achillea* 'Moonshine'
- *Allium christophii*
- *Crambe cordifolia*
- *Diascia* 'Ruby Field'
- *Echinacea purpurea*
- *Euphorbia myrsinites*
- *Gaura lindheimeri*
- *Lavandula intermedia* 'Grosso'
- *Perovskia atriplicifolia*
- *Phlomis fruticosa*
- *Rosmarinus* 'Severn Sea'
- *Sisyrinchium striatum*
- *Verbena bonariensis*

HOT AND DRY PLANTING PROJECT

In this planting scheme, the colours are all pastel shades. Lemon yellows, pinks and pale blues are complemented by silver and glaucous blue foliage.

Ideally, choose a south- or west-facing site for this planting as most drought-tolerant plants prefer a sunny situation. If you have a heavy clay soil, dig it deeply to improve natural drainage and incorporate copious quantities of sharp sand or grit. This will ensure that the top layers of soil, where the roots live, will remain open, well aerated and free draining. A barrowful of sand or grit per square metre is ideal. In a very badly drained site, consider constructing a raised bed if you want to create this garden style.

In a naturally dry garden, use a mulch to retain what little moisture there is. Remember not to plant too deep and to plant slightly above the soil surface to allow for the depth of mulch. Apply a layer of pea gravel or other fine aggregate to a depth of no more than 5cm (2in) spread evenly over the soil between the plants.

KEY TO PLANTING PLAN AND ELEVATION

1 *Lavandula x intermedia* *'Grosso'*
2 *Rosmarinus officinalis* *'Severn Sea'*
3 *Stipa tenuissima*
4 *Gaura lindheimeri*
5 *Pennisetum villosum*
6 *Carex comans* 'Frosted Curls'
7 *Achillea* 'Moonshine'
8 *Festuca glauca* *'Elijah Blue'*
9 *Euphorbia myrsinites*
10 *Helictotrichon sempervirens*
11 *Perovskia atriplicifolia*

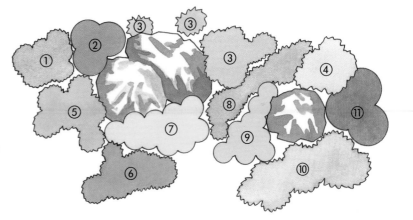

Contemporary Bedding

In recent years, the range of plants available for bedding has expanded enormously, with a whole host of tender perennials, fast-growing hardy perennials and grasses. This new and exciting range of plant material has inspired a fresh look at bedding, and some designers are producing original schemes once again.

The speed of growth and immediate impact of most grasses enables them to compete easily with other bedding subjects. In most cases, grasses can be raised alongside bedding plants in a similar way. Even in winter, some of the evergreen sedges and grasses make excellent bedding subjects, giving far more impact than a traditional scheme of pansies and polyanthus.

Whatever the season, grasses can provide a contrast with other foliage and more flamboyant flowers. This is particularly so with bedding schemes as so many bedding plants are big, brash and bold and make an appealing contrast to the delicate and soft grass foliage.

GRASSES FOR BEDDING
- *Acorus gramineus* 'Ogon'
- *Arundo donax* 'Variegata'
- *Carex* comans 'Bronze Form'
- *Festuca glauca*
- *Helictrotrichon sempervirens*
- *Miscanthus sinensis* 'Morning Light'
- *Uncinia uncinata* 'Rubra

OTHER BEDDING PLANTS
- *Arctotis* 'Flame'
- *Begonia* 'Pin Up Orange'
- *Canna* 'Wyoming'
- *Coleus* 'Juliet Quartermain'
- *Dahlia* 'Moonfire'
- *Fuchsia* 'Thalia'
- *Heuchera* 'Palace Purple'
- *Nicotiana sylvestris*
- *Rudbeckia* 'Goldilocks'

In mixed summer displays, some of the plants will not be hardy and so, in temperate climates, the display will not last through the winter without help. Plants such as begonias are best thrown away and replaced with new plants next year, although the tubers can be dried and kept over winter. Cannas and dahlias will survive over winter if you apply a thick mulch to protect the roots from winter frost. Fuchsias will need to be potted up and kept in a frost-free greenhouse over winter.

To many people, part of the joy of summer bedding is the scope to be creative afresh each year, so most bedding plants are removed and discarded each autumn. If you have included hardy grasses in your display, however, they can be retrieved and planted elsewhere for permanent display.

Left Grasses, herbaceous perennials and traditional bedding plants blend together in this innovative bedding display.

CONTEMPORARY BEDDING PROJECT

This scheme includes a rich combination of orange, bronze, silver and white. The cannas have broad, paddle-shaped leaves in murky brown, and contrast well with the light airy foliage of the white variegated Japanese silver grass (*Miscanthus sinensis* 'Morning Light'). The red hook sedge (*Uncinia uncinata* 'Rubra') is a similar

colour to the begonia, while the blue fescue (*Festuca glauca*) provides a good contrast. This is a summer display and will look attractive from early summer through to autumn.

Most of the grasses in this scheme are hardy so they can be planted in early spring. The giant reed grass (*Arundo donax versicolor*) and the other plants

are tender, so wait to plant them out until all danger of frost has passed in early summer.

Both the cannas and arundo are tall and need to be at the back of the display or they will mask the other plants. Most of these plants will perform best in a rich soil, so prepare the area well and incorporate plenty of compost and a general fertilizer. Although the grasses don't really need this cosseting treatment, it will help them to grow fast and vigorously and perform well.

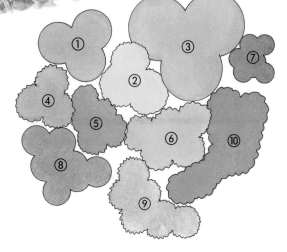

KEY TO PLANTING PLAN AND ELEVATION

1 *Canna* 'Wyoming'
2 *Miscanthus sinensis* 'Morning Light'
3 *Arundo donax versicolor*
4 *Helictrotrichon sempervirens*
5 *Fuchsia* 'Thalia'
6 *Dahlia* 'Moonfire'
7 *Uncinia uncinata* 'Rubra'
8 *Carex comans* 'Bronze Form'
9 *Festuca glauca*
10 *Begonia* 'Pin Up Orange'

Horticultural Showtime

With mixed plantings there are few rules, although the style is usually big and dramatic. By combining shrubs, herbaceous perennials and grasses, sometimes with roses, bulbs and bedding plants, you can achieve a voluptuous effect. Here you have the widest palette of plants from which to choose and the opportunity to select the best of everything.

Mixed borders are most effective on a large scale – try to create good wide borders which are as long as space allows. In such a situation you can explore all the possibilities of the larger grasses in big bold groups.

Below An exuberance of heleniums, rudbeckias and crocosmias softened by wreathes of grasses in this late summer display.

Obviously the size of a border needs to match the scale of the garden and small cameo groups can be very effective. Mixed borders will often have a theme to avoid the overall effect becoming too vague. Perhaps base your display on a colour scheme choosing one or two main colours together with silver and green. Alternatively, plan your border to have a peak display at a particular season.

BACKGROUND SHRUBS FOR A MIXED BORDER

- *Choisya ternata* 'Sundance'
- *Cotinus coggygria* 'Royal Purple'
- *Physocarpus opulifolius* 'Dart's Gold'
- *Rosa* 'Scarlet Fire'

HERBACEOUS AND TENDER PLANTS FOR A MIXED BORDER

- *Achillea* 'Coronation Gold'
- *Anthemis* 'EC Buxton'
- *Canna* 'Assaut'
- *Coreopsis verticillata* 'Grandiflora'
- *Dahlia* 'Bishop of Llandaff'
- *Hemerocallis* 'Chief Sarcoxie'
- *Kniphofia* 'Lord Roberts'
- *Penstemon* 'Rubicundus'
- *Potentilla* 'Gibson's Scarlet'

ORNAMENTAL GRASSES FOR A MIXED BORDER

- *Alopecurus pratensis* 'Aureovariegatus'
- *Chasmanthium latifolium*
- *Cortaderia selloana* 'Aureolineata'
- *Deschampsia cespitosa* 'Goldtau'
- *Festuca glauca* 'Golden Toupee'
- *Hakonechloa macra* 'Aureola'
- *Imperata cylindrica* 'Rubra'
- *Miscanthus sinensis* 'Zebrinus'
- *Pennisetum orientale*
- *Stipa gigantea*

BULBS

Bulbs can be added to mixed borders to add seasonal interest. For spring, choose from tulips, hyacinths, crown imperials (*Fritillaria*) and narcissus. Foxtail lilies (*Eremurus*) are spectacular in early summer, to be replaced with gladioli as the season progresses. Cram them all in for an opulent effect and remember that the dying foliage will be hidden as the grasses and herbaceous plants grow and develop.

HORTICULTURAL SHOWTIME PROJECT

This scheme is based around a mix of golden yellows and rich reds with a peak season of display in mid-summer. The framework of the border is provided by the shrubby plants. The golden Mexican orange blossom (*Choisya ternata* 'Sundance') is evergreen so will also provide some vivid winter colour. The 'Scarlet Fire' rose will not only give a summer display from its flowers but will continue the interest through the winter with bright red hips. The purple smoke bush (*Cotinus coggygria* 'Royal Purple') has ruby foliage throughout the summer and then bold autumn tints. The *Canna*, *Penstemon*, *Dahlia* and *Anthemis* will all give a long season of flower with grasses threaded throughout.

KEY TO PLANTING PLAN AND ELEVATION

1 *Cotinus coggygria* 'Royal Purple'
2 *Rosa* 'Scarlet Fire'
3 *Choisya ternata* 'Sundance'
4 *Canna* 'Assaut'
5 *Miscanthus sinensis* 'Zebrinus'
6 *Dahlia* 'Bishop of Llandaff'
7 *Cortaderia selloana* 'Aureolineata'
8 *Penstemon* 'Rubicundus'
9 *Deschampsia cespitosa* 'Goldtau'
10 *Anthemis* 'EC Buxton'
11 *Festuca glauca* 'Golden Toupee'
12 *Alopecurus pratensis* 'Aureovariegatus'

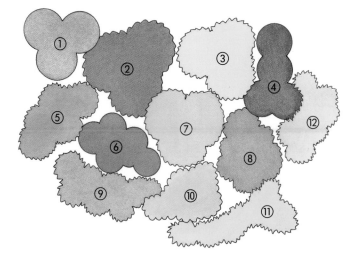

Wild and Woodland Planting

There are grasses for almost all situations and, although most true grasses like an open sunny aspect, some will tolerate a shady site. In addition, sedges and woodrushes thrive in shade, as do bamboos. There are of course degrees of shade and it is important to choose those plants which suit the conditions you can offer, whether it is dry or moist shade.

Shade is often regarded as a problem in a garden but there are many beautiful plants that grow and thrive in shade. Woodland gardens have their own quiet ambience and in low light levels, colours appear more subtle. The delicate foliage of grasses associates well with other shade-loving plants such as ferns, epimediums and hostas. In a woodland garden, grasses carry on the interest in the summer after shrubby species such as camellias and rhododendrons have supplied their dizzy spring and early summer display.

PREPARING A SHADE BED

You will need to prepare the ground well for a shade garden underneath established trees. The roots of the trees are likely to have impoverished the soil so cultivate it well, incorporating generous amounts of compost or other humus. Avoid chopping large roots as this could damage the trees and reduce stability. An annual feed and mulch will considerably encourage growth in these situations. To keep the natural effect, edge woodland paths with natural cut logs or branches and surface them with woodchips.

Left Many grasses and sedges, such as Bowles' golden sedge thrive in light shade provided by trees, such as these silver birch.

WOODLAND GRASSES
- *Acorus gramineus* 'Ogon'
- *Arrhenatherum elatius bulbosum* 'Variegatum'
- *Carex morrowii* 'Variegata'
- *Chasmanthium latifolium*
- *Deschampsia cespitosa*
- *Deschampsia flexuosa*
- *Hakonechloa macra* 'Aureola'
- *Imperata cylindrica* 'Rubra'
- *Luzula sylvatica* 'Aurea'
- *Millium effusum* 'Aureum'
- *Ophiopogon planiscapus* 'Nigrescens'
- *Phalaris arundinacea* 'Feesey'
- *Poa chaixii*

OTHER WOODLAND PLANTS
- *Ajuga reptans* 'Catlin's Giant'
- *Alchemilla mollis*
- *Aruncus dioicus*
- *Asplenium scolopendrium* 'Crispum'
- *Bergenia* 'Ballawley'
- *Brunnera macrophylla* 'Hadspen Cream'
- *Epimedium perralderianum*
- *Euphorbia amygdaloides robbiae*
- *Lamium maculatum* 'Beacon Silver'
- *Ligularia przewalskii*
- *Liriope muscari*
- *Onoclea sensibilis*
- *Polystichum setiferum*
- *Pulmonaria saccharata* 'Argentea'

WILD AND WOODLAND PLANTING PROJECT

The general effect of this planting is soft, gentle and muted as all the plants are pale in colour. Throughout the season a background of soft greens and creams will be highlighted with touches of other colours. Most of the grasses are compact so the ligularia and goat's beard (*Aruncus*) are included to give some contrasting height.

This is another planting where bulbs could be added to great effect. In the spring miniature daffodils, crocuses, dog's tooth violets (*Erythronium*), grape hyacinths (*Muscari*) and wood anemones (*Anemone nemorosa*) could provide a sheet of colour among the emerging grass shoots. These bulbs would all have to be planted in the autumn. Later subjects, such as lilies, would provide a stunning display in mid-summer above the grasses.

KEY TO PLANTING PLAN AND ELEVATION

1 *Epimedium perralderianum*
2 *Imperata cylindrica* 'Rubra'
3 *Aruncus dioicus*
4 *Carex morrowii* 'Variegata'
5 *Ligularia przewalskii*
6 *Chasmanthium latifolium*
7 *Bergenia* 'Ballawley'
8 *Deschampsia flexuosa*
9 *Brunnera macrophylla* 'Hadspen Cream'
10 *Luzula sylvatica* 'Aurea'
11 *Euphorbia amygdaloides robbiae*

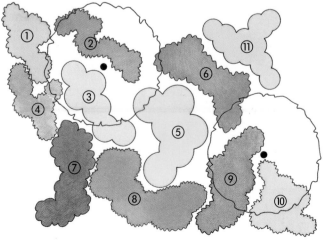

Bamboos and Biggies

Most bamboos have relatively small and narrow foliage, so the best plants to contrast with them are those with big dramatic leaves. Most large-leaved plants hold their foliage horizontally and this contrasts well with the predominantly vertical habit of most bamboos. There are many hardy and tender plants with large leaves.

Creating such a dramatic scheme will require a fair amount of space as most large-leaved plants are vigorous. The individual plants should be given enough room to develop properly. Groundcover bamboos, such as *Pleioblastus auricomus*, can be allowed to romp away underneath the bigger subjects, covering the ground in a contrasting carpet of tiny golden leaves.

Many tender plants with big leaves contrast and associate well with bamboos. Bananas and cannas are familiar to most gardeners; then there is *Sparrmannia africana*. This grows to 3m (10ft) in a season, with giant dinner plate hairy leaves and clusters of delicate white flowers; just the thing to grow alongside a black bamboo (*Phyllostachys nigra*). All these will need winter protection if they are to survive until the next season.

A contemporary scheme such as this will benefit from additional 'props' to enhance the setting – large lumps of driftwood or gnarled wood stumps for example.

Above These potted bamboos, grasses and other plants can be rearranged or added to, providing infinite opportunities for change.

BIG-LEAVED PLANTS

- *Abutilon vitifolium*
- *Aralia elata*
- *Bergenia* 'Ballawley'
- *Canna* 'Wyoming'
- *Catalpa bignoniodes* 'Aurea'
- *Crambe cordifolia*
- *Dahlia imperialis*
- *Ensete ventricosa*
- *Fatsia japonica*
- *Hedychium densiflorum*
- *Hosta* 'Frances Williams'
- *Mahonia japonica*
- *Melianthus major*
- *Musa basjoo*
- *Paulownia tomentosa*
- *Rheum palmatum* 'Atrosanguineum'
- *Rhus typhina*
- *Ricinus* 'Carmencita'
- *Sparrmannia africana*
- *Tetrapanax papyrifer*

BAMBOOS TO ACCOMPANY BIG-LEAVED PLANTS

- *Chusquea culeo*
- *Fargesia murieliae*
- *Fargesia nitida*
- *Phyllostachys aurea*
- *Phyllostachys nigra*
- *Phyllostachys vivax* 'Aureocaulis'
- *Pleioblastus auricomus*
- *Pleioblastus pygmaeus*
- *Pleioblastus shibuyans* 'Tsuboi'
- *Pleioblastus variegatus*
- *Pseudosasa japonica*
- *Sasa veitchii*
- *Thamnocalamus crassinodus* 'Kew Beauty'

BAMBOOS AND BIGGIES PROJECT

Bamboos are the key plants in this project, but the companion plants are shrubs and herbaceous subjects with large leaves. Most of the bamboos have green foliage. The golden Indian bean tree (*Catalpa bignoniodes* 'Aurea') will give glowing golden summer colour and tone nicely with the gold culms of

Phyllostachys vivax 'Aureocaulis'. Large leaves and brilliant orange autumn tints are the main feature of the sumach (*Rhus typhina*), while the mahonia has sweetly scented yellow flowers over glossy green foliage in mid winter. Such a scheme has interest throughout the year.

Be sure to remove the lower foliage from the black and golden bamboos to show off the culm colours. You can also cut the golden Indian Bean tree (*Catalpa bignonioides* 'Aurea') back hard each spring and feed generously to encourage vigorous growth and huge leaves. *Paulownia* can be treated the same way.

KEY TO PLANTING PLAN AND ELEVATION

1   *Rhus typhina*
2   *Phyllostachys vivax* 'Aureocaulis'
3   *Pseudosasa japonica*
4   *Mahonia japonica*
5   *Phyllostachys nigra*
6   *Pleioblastus auricomus*
7   *Rheum palmatum* 'Atrosanguineum'
8   *Sasa veitchii*
9   *Catalpa bignoniodes* 'Aurea'
10 *Bergenia* 'Ballawley'
11 *Hosta* 'Frances Williams'

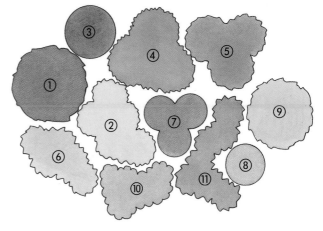

Wet Feet Grasses

Although most grasses are natives of dry situations, most sedges and rushes grow and thrive in damper conditions, often by a stream or pool. Water in the garden is a very horizontal element in the landscape and the vertical foliage of sedges and rushes is displayed perfectly in such a setting. Still water often has a mirror-like quality, so the effect of the plants will be doubled with the added value of reflections.

Some of these plants may be true marginal plants, actually growing within a pond or stream with water over the crown. Others will prefer to grow within the adjacent boggy soil that is constantly moist. If you are lucky enough to have a natural stream or pond then you will probably have a variety of different habitats in which to grow such moisture lovers.

If you have a more formal pool that is lined with concrete or butyl, such marginals can be grown in baskets and supported on bricks at their ideal depth. Most marginals such as *Glyceria maxima variegata* and *Typha minima* will only want a few inches of water over their crowns. The true bog species such as *Carex*, *Juncus* and *Cyperus* species will want constantly moist soil. This can be created with a drip irrigation system or by constructing a pond so that there is a very slight overflow. Lining an area with polythene will also help to retain moisture.

As with most other planting schemes, the most attractive results are often achieved using combinations of grasses and other plants.

POOLSIDE GRASSES
- *Acorus calamus* 'Argenteostriatus'
- *Carex elata* 'Aurea'
- *Carex morrowii* 'Variegata'
- *Carex pendula*
- *Cyperus longus*
- *Equisetum hyemale*
- *Glyceria maxima variegata*
- *Juncus effusus* 'Spiralis'
- *Schoenoplectus* subsp *tabernaemontani* 'Zebrinus'
- *Typha minima*

OTHER MARGINALS AND AQUATICS
- *Caltha palustris* 'Flore Plena'
- *Hosta* 'Aureomarginata'
- *Lysichiton americanus*
- *Mimulus guttatus*
- *Nymphaea* 'Froebelii'
- *Primula florindae*
- *Rheum palmatum* 'Atrosanguineum'
- *Rodgersia podophylla*
- *Scrophularia auriculata* 'Variegata'

Left This lush waterside planting includes many reeds and sedges which thrive in the constantly damp soil at the poolside.

WET FEET GRASSES PLANTING PROJECT

This project has many different aquatic plants both within and alongside the water. The sedges, rushes and other marginals are part of the 'supporting cast', clothing the banks of the pool. However, the upright and stark features of *Glyceria maxima variegata* and *Typha minima* are the stars of the show, emerging from the midst of the still water and contrasted by the flat round leaves of the water lily. This is all very gentle and natural and would fit in with a cottage style garden. The fluffy groups blend into each other in a relaxed way. A formal pool would call for a more dramatic treatment with bolder groups and less variety. Each group would make a strong statement on its own.

KEY TO PLANTING PLAN AND ELEVATION

1   *Carex elata* 'Aurea'
2   *Hosta* 'Aureomarginata'
3   *Cyperus longus*
4   *Rheum palmatum*
    'Atrosanguineum'
5   *Rodgersia podophylla*
6   *Nymphaea* 'Froebelii'

7   *Typha minima*
8   *Carex pendula*
9   *Juncus effusus* 'Spiralis'
10 *Acorus calamus*
    'Argenteostriatus'
11 *Glyceria maxima variegata*

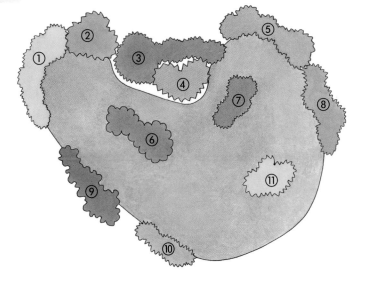

Spiky Companions

There is something quite bewitching about spiky plants, plants with narrow, vertical and pointed leaves. Of course most grasses fall into this category, everything from the chubby little hedgehogs through to huge bristling monsters. On top of that there are those with a softer, floppier appearance but they are still all 'spikies' at heart.

Although I have emphasized the value of contrasting different types of foliage and flowers with grasses and bamboos, it can sometimes be very effective to use a whole range of spiky plants together in an extravaganza of the perpendicular. Many spiky plants have a certain presence about them, a dominant almost aggressive appearance that draws the eye. This is why they are so effective in planting schemes.

To create a spiky scheme, choose grasses with strong, stiff outlines rather than the softer weeping types, although these could be used for a gentler effect. Spiky planting conjures up an almost Wild West atmosphere so you could mulch the soil between the plants with gravel or even sand with boulders or bleached wood. Maybe you could include an old decaying cartwheel obtained from a bygones shop or a farm sale.

Care must be taken with some spiky plants. Agave and Yucca both have needle-sharp tips to the leaves. Care must be taken when working around them not to cause a puncture wound or eye injury. If you have small children I would advise you to cut off the tips.

Right The *Agave americana* 'Variegata' is a nice addition to a group of spiky plants but must be overwintered in frost-free conditions.

SPIKY GRASSES
- *Acorus gramineus* 'Ogon'
- *Carex oshimensis* 'Evergold'
- *Cortaderia richardii*
- *Festuca glauca*
- *Helictotrichon sempervirens*
- *Luzula sylvatica* 'Aurea'
- *Miscanthus sinensis* 'Morning Light'
- *Molinia caerulea* 'Variegata'
- *Stipa gigantea*
- *Uncinia uncinata rubra*

OTHER SPIKY PLANTS
- *Agapanthus* 'Headbourne Hybrids'
- *Agave americana* (tender)
- *Astelia chathamica*
- *Beschorneria yuccoides* (tender)
- *Cordyline australis*
- *Ophiopogon planiscapus* 'Nigrescens'
- *Phormium tenax* 'Purpureum'
- *Yucca flaccida* 'Golden Sword'
- *Yucca flaccida* 'Ivory'

SPIKY COMPANIONS PLANTING PROJECT

As well as grasses, this planting scheme uses New Zealand flax (*Phormium tenax*) which is available in green, purple and various variegations. The leaves are all long and narrow, originating from ground level, and sometimes the plants produce lofty flowering spikes. The purple variety used in this example will contrast well with the dreamy white foliage of *Miscanthus sinensis* 'Morning Light'.

Then there are yuccas with thick and chunky pointed leaves. The most common colour is a glaucous green, although there are several variegated types such as the *Yucca flaccida* 'Golden Sword' used here. The cabbage palm (*Cordyline australis*) is on the borderline of hardiness but where they manage to survive in sheltered sites they can eventually become small trees with tall stems and heads like palms, hence the common name. In an exposed site, protect cordylines over winter by bunching the foliage together and wrapping with soft string. This will protect the growing point and young foliage.

This scheme also includes the silvery *Astelia chathamica* which will contrast with the black strap-like leaves of *Ophiopogon planiscapus* 'Nigrescens'.

KEY TO PLANTING PLAN AND ELEVATION

1 *Cordyline australis*
2 *Miscanthus sinensis* 'Morning Light'
3 *Phormium tenax* 'Purpureum'
4 *Helictotrichon sempervirens*
5 *Yucca flaccida* 'Golden Sword'
6 *Astelia chathamica*
7 *Acorus gramineus* 'Ogon'
8 *Stipa gigantea*
9 *Festuca glauca*
10 *Ophiopogon planiscapus* 'Nigrescens'

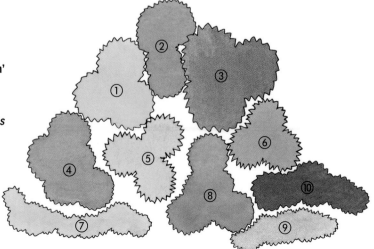

Pots and Planters

Containers act as focal points within a garden, rather like pieces of sculpture, but each can display a perfect planting scheme in miniature. Too often, however, container planting schemes draw attention because of their poor quality and the whole value is lost. Design each as a little masterpiece and nurture with love and care.

Pots and planters may be simple and functional in style, such as a plain terracotta pot. Plain planters act as a foil for the plants they contain, which can be dramatic and complex. In other cases the container itself may be the star and the planting merely the supporting act that accompanies it. Here the planting will need to be restrained and quiet so that it does not compete with the container. Either way, plants and container should provide a unique little cameo within a garden, to be enjoyed for the detail they provide.

Below This old, rusted chain makes an original container for this grass and contrasts well with the snowy white stones.

Most grasses and bamboos can be grown in containers, although the size of the plants must relate to the size of the container. A small planter of 50cm (20in) in diameter will probably take one large grass or three smaller ones. These will grow happily for two or three years before they need to be divided and repotted.

Plants in containers are usually arranged closer together than those in the open ground to get a quick effect, but the lifespan of the display will be shorter. Some people may prefer to grow grasses individually in pots, displayed on a terrace or gravel area. These can be arranged and rearranged as the season develops to provide a constantly changing and ever-fresh display.

GLITZY GRASSES AND BRASSY BAMBOOS FOR PLAIN PLANTERS

- *Arundo donax versicolor*
- *Carex comans* 'Bronze Form'
- *Carex elata* 'Aurea'
- *Carex oshimensis* 'Evergold'
- *Carex phyllocephala* 'Sparkler'
- *Hakonechloa macra* 'Aureola'
- *Miscanthus sinensis* 'Cosmopolitan'
- *Pennisetum setaceum* 'Rubrum'
- *Phalaris arundinacea* 'Feesey'
- *Phyllostachys nigra*
- *Phyllostachys vivax* 'Aureocaulis'
- *Pleioblastus auricomus*

PLAIN JANES FOR SOPHISTICATED CONTAINERS

- *Briza maxima*
- *Cortaderia selloana* 'Pumila'
- *Deschampsia cespitosa*
- *Miscanthus sinensis* 'Gracillimus'
- *Panicum virgatum*
- *Pennisetum alopecuroides*
- *Stipa tenuissima*

POTS AND PLANTERS PLANTING PROJECT

Make sure the containers have good drainage, with holes at the bottom to allow excess water to drain away. A layer of rough compost, gravel or stones at the base of the container will help to keep this drainage channel open. The rest of the container should be filled with a proprietary soil-based potting compost. This will last better than a soil-less or peat-based compost which will become compact and stay too wet in winter. Grasses can also be top-heavy and blow over, so a weighty compost will add stability.

After planting the grasses into the pots, there is no reason why the compost surface cannot be topped with cobbles, pebbles, bark chippings or sea shells to enhance the effect and to retain soil moisture. Don't forget to water and feed regularly.

KEY TO PLANTING PLAN AND ELEVATION

1   *Canna* 'Champigny'
2   *Phalaris arundinacea* 'Feesey'
3   *Pennisetum setaceum* 'Rubrum'
4   *Helichrysum petiolare*
5   *Festuca glauca* 'Elijah Blue'
6   *Osteospermum* 'James Elliman'
7   *Abutilon* 'Cannington Peter'
8   *Carex elata* 'Aurea'
9   *Coleus* 'Juliet Quartermain'
10 *Acorus gramineus* 'Ogon'
11 *Verbena* 'Quartz Red'

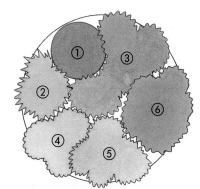

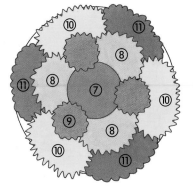

Day and Night

A short while ago I had the opportunity to contribute a planting scheme to a Millennium Garden with a time theme. The centrepiece is a flower garden and it seemed appropriate to follow the time theme by dividing the borders into day and night areas. The daytime bed is a mixture of bright sunny colours – yellows, oranges and reds – while the night border is a mix of dark blues, silvers and whites – the colours of moonlight.

Designing a planting scheme using a colour theme is a common technique that many garden designer's frequently use. Gertrude Jekyll, a famous designer in the early twentieth century often planned themed borders. A whole area may be planned using just one colour and shrubs, herbaceous plants, grasses and bulbs chosen to tie in with the theme. More complex schemes may use more than one colour, for example blue and yellow, or apricot, bronze and purple. Very subtle schemes may use particular shades such as lemon yellow and dark blue. There are endless options.

Clever colour schemes can change with the season, so a large border may be planned so that all the spring flowers are in pastel shades – pinks, primrose and pale blue. Later in the season as new plants come into their peak, the colours could be hot yellows, orange and red.

Ornamental grasses fit in well with so many colour schemes as most grasses are neutral. Green, silver or white foliage can be used with almost any combination although the yellow variegations will have to be used with more care. Green grasses have a very calming effect within a colour scheme, particularly with hot or strident colours such as red, orange or purple. Silver and white variegated grasses add lightness and will be valuable used with dark blues or rich reds.

Left In mid-summer ornamental grasses are valuable constituents of this colourful day and night garden.

PLANTS FOR 'SUNSHINE' PLANTING

- Achillea 'Coronation Gold'
- Alopecurus pratensis 'Aureomarginatus'
- Cortaderia selloana 'Gold Band'
- Festuca glauca 'Golden Toupee'
- Hakonechloa macra 'Aureola'
- Hemerocallis 'Stafford'
- Penstemon 'Garnet'
- Potentilla 'Gibson's Scarlet'
- Pleioblastus auricomus

PLANTS FOR 'MOONLIGHT' PLANTING

- Aconitum 'Bressingham Spire'
- Festuca glauca 'Elijah's Blue'
- Miscanthus sinensis 'Morning Light'
- Molinia caerulea 'Variegata'
- Ophiopogon planiscapus 'Nigrescens'
- Penstemon 'White Bedder'
- Pleioblastus variegatus
- Salvia uliginosa

DAY AND NIGHT PLANTING PROJECT

Grasses fit beautifully into this scheme and the sunshine planting includes golden grasses such as the tufty golden foxtail grass (*Alopecurus pratensis* 'Aureovariegatus'), golden Hakone grass (*Hakonechloa macra* 'Aureola') and the striking golden pampas (*Cortaderia selloana* 'Aureolineata'). Herbaceous perennials in the sunshine planting include *Penstemon* 'Garnet', *Coreopsis verticillata* and the red day lily (*Hemerocallis* 'Stafford'). You could add many other hot-coloured herbaceous plants to extend the effect. The shrubby spindle bush with golden foliage (*Euonymus fortunei* 'Emerald 'n' Gold') fills the corners to provide a touch of winter colour from its evergreen foliage.

The moonlight planting features white variegated grasses such as Japanese silver grass (*Miscanthus sinensis* 'Morning Light'), the diminutive false oat grass (*Arrhenatherum elatius bulbosum* 'Variegatum'), and the striped purple moor grass (*Molinia caerulea* 'Variegata'). These touches of moonlight are contrasted by the deep blues of monkshood (*Aconitum* 'Bressingham Spire'), the familiar blue cranesbill (*Geranium* 'Johnson's Blue') and the almost black foliage of *Ophiopogon planiscapus* 'Nigrescens'.

KEY TO PLANTING PLAN AND ELEVATION

1 *Alopecurus pratensis* 'Aureovariegatus'
2 *Coreopsis verticillata*
3 *Penstemon* 'Garnet' ('Andenken an Friedrich Hahn')
4 *Hemerocallis* 'Stafford'
5 *Cortaderia selloana* 'Aureolineata'
6 *Hakonechloa macra* 'Aureola'
7 *Euonymus fortunei* 'Emerald 'n' Gold'
8 *Festuca glauca* 'Golden Toupee'
9 *Pleioblastus auricomus*
10 *Alchemilla mollis*

11 *Arrhenatherum elatius bulbosum* 'Variegatum'
12 *Molinia caerulea* 'Variegata'
13 *Artemesia stelleriana* 'Boughton Silver'
14 *Ophiopogon planiscapus* 'Nigrescens'
15 *Miscanthus sinensis* 'Morning Light'
16 *Geranium* 'Johnson's Blue'
17 *Pleioblastus variegatus*
18 *Aconitum* 'Bressingham Spire'
19 *Euonymus fortunei* 'Emerald Gaiety'
20 *Festuca glauca* 'Elijah Blue'

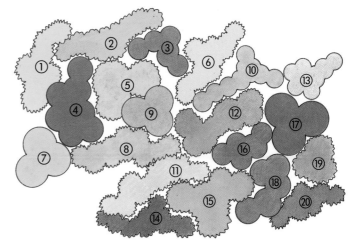

Cool Blue

Grasses lend themselves to many different colour schemes, but one obvious feature to exploit is the handsome glaucous blue foliage of many varieties of grass and bamboo. Blue is a very valuable colour in the garden and there are many beautiful shrubs and herbaceous plants with blue flowers which will enhance the effect.

In any single colour scheme, avoid choosing plants of exactly the same colour or the effect will be monotonous – it is important to introduce a little variation to keep things interesting. For example, in a blue scheme, a little silver foliage will go a long way to lifting the effect and really enhancing the blues. Try to choose a range of tones and tints within your colour band; include some light blues, vivid blues and even some purple-blues.

Varying the height and shape of plants can also help to keep a grouping interesting. Make sure there are upright

BLUE GRASSES
- *Festuca glauca* 'Elijah Blue'
- *Helictotrichon sempervirens*
- *Koeleria glauca*
- *Leymus arenarius*
- *Panicum virgatum* 'Prairie Sky'
- *Phyllostachys nigra*

OTHER BLUE PLANTS
- *Acanthus spinosus*
- *Anchusa azurea* 'Loddon Royalist'
- *Astelia chathamica*
- *Ceanothus* 'Blue Mound'
- *Cerinthe major* 'Purpurascens'
- *Eryngium variifolium*
- *Melianthus major*
- *Ophiopogon planiscapus* 'Nigrescens'
- *Perovskia atriplicifolia* 'Blue Spire'
- *Salvia uliginosa*
- *Yucca flaccida* 'Ivory'

shapes as well as rounded mounds, spiky plants to contrast with softer forms, and a selection of different heights to make a pleasing overall effect.

The individual plants in an all-blue scheme link together in a cool and subtle way, but you could introduce an added punch with just a touch of a rich, hot colour. Perhaps the orange of a red hot poker such as *Kniphofia rooperi*, or the dark red tones of *Crocosmia* 'Lucifer'. Although they do not literally fit in with the colour scheme, such unexpected and contrasting touches can make the difference between a nice planting and a stunning display.

Left Ornamental onions grow alongside blue grasses in this modern minimalist garden with its stone sculpture centrepiece.

COOL BLUE PLANTING PROJECT

The bones of this planting are a tall clump of black bamboo and a stark chunky group of yuccas. As well as the glaucous blue grasses, we have broader glaucous foliage from the *Melianthus* and *Yucca*.

The *Perovskia* provides fine elegant spires of wonderful pale blue flowers in late summer and also has grey foliage. In a good, warm season and a sheltered spot, the *Melianthus* will produce lovely soft brick-red flowers in mid-autumn, contrasting well with the cool blues.

The black culms of the bamboo are picked up by the dark *Ophiopogon* leaves at the front of the display. In some years, the yucca will produce a huge white flower spike in late summer but even if it doesn't the architectural foliage is of immense value. Although peaking in late summer and autumn, this scheme has interest throughout the year, particularly as most of the grasses are evergreen.

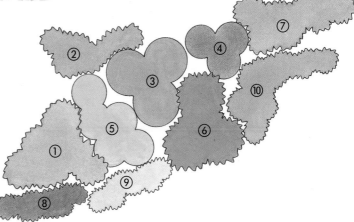

KEY TO PLANTING PLAN AND ELEVATION

1 *Helictotrichon sempervirens*
2 *Leymus arenarius*
3 *Phyllostachys nigra*
4 *Perovskia atriplicifolia* 'Blue Spire'
5 *Melianthus major*
6 *Yucca flaccida* 'Ivory'
7 *Panicum virgatum* 'Prairie Sky'
8 *Ophiopogon planiscapus* 'Nigrescens'
9 *Festuca glauca* 'Elijah Blue'
10 *Koeleria glauca*

All Green

The value of green is often overlooked in the garden; it is seen as a neutral colour, almost a non colour. Providing you choose plants with lots of other interesting characteristics, such as bold foliage and strong shapes, you can create a dramatic scheme using green alone. Of course there are many shades of green, so avoid the monotony by selecting plants with as many different greens as possible.

Obviously many grasses are predominantly green, but the shades of green vary hugely, as do the habits and shapes of the plants. *Panicum virgatum* is grey-green with small leaves and a very upright habit. *Stipa tenuissima* is soft green with an almost trailing habit. *Pennisetum alopecuroides* has slightly wider leaves and is bright apple green. For some contrast in height we could add *Miscanthus sinensis* 'Gracillimus' and *Arundo donax*. The latter also has huge blue-green leaves.

There are many other interesting foliage plants, apart from grasses, which can benefit an all-green scheme. Many bamboos, including *Fargesia murieliae* and *Pseudosasa japonica*, are predominantly green and will fit in perfectly. Plants with huge leaves such as elephant's ears (*Bergenia*) or *Fatsia japonica* with its glossy green leaves can be used. If the situation is damp enough, include a few hostas and ferns as wonderful green foliage additions.

GREEN GRASSES
- *Arundo donax*
- *Miscanthus sinensis* 'Gracillimus'
- *Panicum virgatum*
- *Pennisetum alopecuroides*
- *Stipa tenuissima*

GREEN BAMBOOS
- *Chusquea culeou*
- *Fargesia murieliae*
- *Pleioblastus pygmaeus*
- *Pseudosasa japonica*

OTHER GREEN FOLIAGE
- *Aralia elata*
- *Bergenia* 'Morgenröte'
- *Cordyline australis*
- *Fatsia japonica*
- *Hedera helix* 'Manda's Crested'
- *Hosta lancifolia*
- *Mahonia japonica*
- *Thymus serpyllum* 'Annie Hall'
- *Viburnum davidii*
- *Yucca gloriosa*

Right The lime greens of euphorbias and hostas tie in well with grasses to give a lush, all-green effect in this garden.

ALL GREEN PLANTING PROJECT

This scheme makes use of an interesting selection of green foliage. Some plants do have green flowers that would fit in well, but it is green leaves that make up this planting. Some of the plants I have chosen will flower at some point in the year. If you want to be purist and maintain the green-only theme throughout the year, remove the flowers and keep to just green.

However, a touch of colour amongst all that green can be quite stunning. You can actually engineer that further by purposely including such touches. For example, a group of deep red tulips could provide a brilliant splash of contrasting colour in the spring which will actually enhance the green foliage. A lily such as 'Fire King' would carry the touch of red into early summer. This could be followed by a red canna such as 'President'.

TOUCHES OF RED
- *Canna* 'President'
- *Crocosmia* 'Lucifer'
- *Hemerocallis* 'Stafford'
- *Lilium* 'Fire King'
- *Papaver orientale* 'Beauty of Livermere'
- *Penstemon* 'Chester Scarlet
- *Tulipa* 'Oxford'

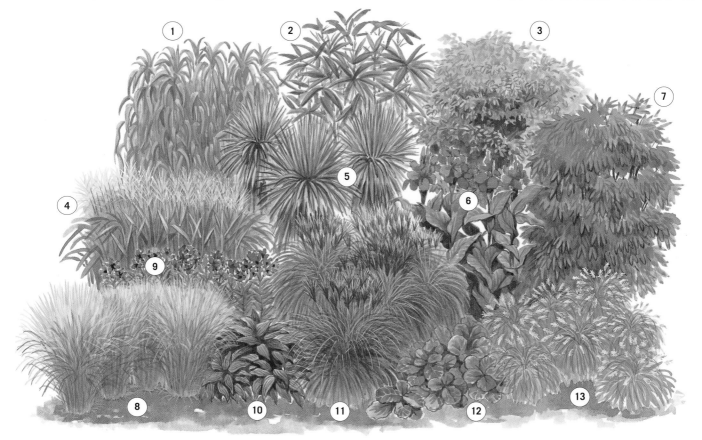

KEY TO PLANTING PLAN AND ELEVATION

1 *Arundo donax*
2 *Pseudosasa japonica*
3 *Aralia elata*
4 *Panicum virgatum*
5 *Cordyline australis*
6 *Canna* 'President'
7 *Fargesia murieliae*
8 *Stipa tenuissima*
9 *Lilium* 'Fire King'
10 *Hosta lancifolia*
11 *Miscanthus sinensis* 'Gracillimus'
12 *Bergenia* 'Morgenröte'
13 *Pennisetum alopecuroides*

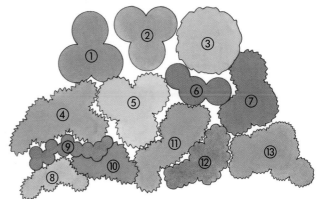

Final Fling

Suddenly in late summer we are reminded that autumn is coming and shorter days, chilly mornings and the extra dew on the lawn all point to the demise of the sunny days. For some, autumn is a melancholy time in preparation for the winter. However, you can make a glorious grand finale out of the many garden plants that are at their peak in late summer and autumn.

Many of the grasses are, of course, at their best at this time of year as the fluffy plumes and flower-heads come into their own. As always, they associate well with other plants and the best displays are those that make an eclectic mix of all that's best in autumn colour.

Little cameo plantings are always a joy. The cut-leaved sumach (*Rhus typhina* 'Dissecta') is often grown for its vivid red autumn tints. Why not set it off with a sea of frothy oatmeal-coloured *Deschampsia cespitosa*? This plant provides interest all the year, but peaks to a wonderful autumn crescendo.

There is a danger that any planting scheme designed for one peak season can be dreary for the rest of the year. However, with careful choice of plants it is possible to create a mixed border that looks good all the year and builds to a blaze of glory in the autumn months. Grasses are very useful in achieving this, carrying on the display right into winter.

GRASSES FOR AUTUMN
- *Cortaderia selloana*
- *Imperata cylindrica* 'Rubra'
- *Miscanthus sinensis* 'Silberfeder'
- *Miscanthus sinensis* 'Zebrinus'
- *Panicum virgatum* 'Heavy Metal'
- *Pennisetum alopecuroides* 'Hameln'
- *Pennisetum setaceum* 'Rubrum'
- *Spartina pectinata*

OTHER PLANTS FOR AUTUMN
- *Aconitum napellus*
- *Canna* 'President'
- *Cotinus coggygria* 'Royal Purple'
- *Dahlia* 'Bishop of Llandaff'
- *Kniphofia rooperi*
- *Perovskia atriplicifolia* 'Blue Spire'
- *Rhus typhina* 'Dissecta'
- *Rosa* 'Geranium'
- *Sedum spectabile*

Left Regal flower spikes of pampas tower above dark red cannas in this dramatic planting at Longwood Gardens in Pennsylvania, USA.

FINAL FLING PLANTING PROJECT

In this planting, the glow of autumn flowers mixes with the plump rose hips and the rich tints of the smoke bush (*Cotinus*), giving a glorious late display. However, there will be interest throughout the season from the grass foliage and that of the *Cotinus*. The rose has early flowers before the hips and the cannas and dahlias will bloom throughout the summer. For added interest, include some spring bulbs such as narcissus and tulips. The dominant colour scheme is warm autumnal reds and oranges, with touches of icy blue.

KEY TO PLANTING PLAN AND ELEVATION

1. *Cortaderia selloana*
2. *Cotinus coggygria* 'Royal Purple'
3. *Rosa* 'Geranium'
4. *Aconitum napellus*
5. *Canna* 'President'
6. *Kniphofia rooperi*
7. *Imperata cylindrica* 'Rubra'
8. *Miscanthus sinensis* 'Silberfeder'
9. *Sedum spectabile*
10. *Dahlia* 'Bishop of Llandaff'
11. *Panicum virgatum* 'Heavy Metal'

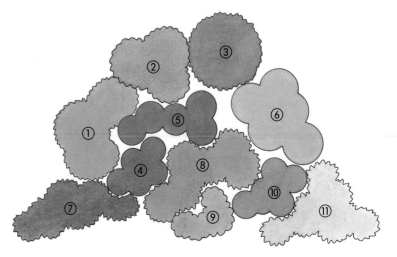

5 | OTHER SCENARIOS

Right Although not normally grown as a waterside plant, this pampas grass (*Cortaderia selloana*) looks perfectly at home in its poolside location.

Centre Stage

As well as slotting in perfectly with other plants in so many situations in the garden, grasses and bamboos have enough character and presence to stand alone as specimen plants. They can be used as individuals set in small beds in lawns, or in gravel gardens, or as highlights in borders of low plants.

When grasses and bamboos are grown on their own as specimen plants, the lack of competition around them enables the plants to grow to their ultimate shape and size. It is then that their true elegance and impact can be seen and we can really appreciate them for the beautiful plants they are. A specimen grass or bamboo set on its own can be a stunning feature.

BOLD BAMBOOS

A good specimen plant will have a long season of interest. Bamboos are the perfect choice as they are evergreen and have a permanent woody framework. Oriental gardens often feature single specimens of bamboo with nothing more than raked gravel and rocks around them.

Bamboos are excellent as specimens because they present an elegant statement as soon as they are planted, which will continue to grow and develop. Almost all

SPECIMEN BAMBOOS

- *Chusquea culeou*
- *Fargesia nitida* 'Nymphenburg'
- *Phyllostachys nigra*
- *Pseudosasa japonica*

SPECIMEN GRASSES

- *Arundo donax*
- *Cortaderia richardii*
- *Cortaderia selloana*
- *Cortaderia selloana* 'Aureolineata'
- *Cortaderia selloana* 'Silver Fountain'
- *Helictotrichon sempervirens*
- *Miscanthus sinensis condensatus* 'Cosmopolitan'
- *Pennisetum setaceum* 'Rubrum'
- *Spartina pectinata* 'Aureomarginata'
- *Stipa gigantea*

bamboos could be grown as specimens but the more vigorous and coarser types are probably best avoided in favour of the more select and slower-growing varieties.

GRASSES WITH PRESENCE

Grasses need a little more careful selection as many are herbaceous and die back in the winter months. Care must be taken to choose those that are either evergreen, or provide valuable and handsome winter structure, despite the fact that they have turned brown.

Pampas grass (*Cortaderia selloana*) is probably the best-known of all grasses for use as a specimen plant. Despite its old-fashioned feel, it is still a superb plant for creating a bold statement in a garden. It is evergreen and has superb, long-lasting flower spikes of immense proportions. There are only a few weeks in late winter and early spring when it may look untidy. There are many forms and cultivars, including variegated forms such as 'Aureolineata' and 'Silver Fountain'. In addition, there are other good evergreen grasses, with strong bold shapes that will make a good exclamation.

Left Pampas grass (*Cortaderia selloana*), makes a spectacular and long-lived display as a specimen plant.

Meadows and Lawns

Meadow gardening is usually inspired by conservation and native species. However, at its simplest, it is nothing more than a patch of grass, large or small, with other flowering plants mixed in.

By avoiding fertilizers and weedkillers, we can encourage a wider range of grasses and wildflowers. This in turn will support a wider range of birds, insects and other fauna.

A wildflower meadow can be created by sowing a suitable mix of grass and wildflowers, or by leaving lawn areas to grow without regular mowing. When sowing meadow seed, it is essential to choose a seed mix suitable for the site, whether it is wet or dry, acid or alkaline, sunny or shaded.

Annual meadows are sown from a mixture of species, such as poppies, cornflowers and corn marigolds which would naturally have lived in cornfields. Such mixtures will only thrive in freshly cultivated soils so they will need to be sown afresh each year. A mixture of cornfield annuals and grasses will give a colourful display in the first year before the grasses and perennial plants take over for future years.

ONE STEP FURTHER

Some gardeners will want to enhance this effect adding specific plants to a meadow area. Bulbs are the obvious example and crocus, narcissus and even tulips can be naturalized within grass. If conditions are right, rarer plants such as native orchids and fritillaries might be grown, giving added conservation value.

Adventurous gardeners may wish to blur the edges between meadow and prairie gardening by adding exotic plants to an existing grass sward. An area of rough grass could be interplanted with huge clumps of pampas grass (*Cortaderia selloana*) for example, making a superb autumn statement. Or perhaps plant some blue cranesbill (*Geranium* 'Johnson's Blue') in amongst the grass. There is a wild blue cranesbill that grows effectively in grass verges so it is not surprising that this similar cultivated species is successful. These and many other tough herbaceous plants could be added to meadow grass areas.

Above Annual rudbeckias grown amongst grasses make an innovative meadow, but the display will last only a single season.

MEADOW MAINTENANCE

Meadows are usually cut once a year in mid- to late summer, however grass with late species must be left for a single cut in early autumn. All the cuttings should be removed to reduce the fertility of the soil and encourage a greater diversity of plants. The timing of this cut needs to be adjusted to the flowering period of the species present. Allow them to set and distribute seed before you cut off the seed-heads.

Hedges and Edges

Grasses and bamboos might be considered as poor plants for making hedges and edges as they are not naturally formal. But they do have their uses for creating interesting screens and neat edgings to beds and borders.

USING BAMBOOS

Bamboos can be used as a hedge or screen quite effectively. One would not normally trim them, although it is possible. The trimmed effect is, however, not very attractive and destroys the natural graceful outline of the plant. If you want a clipped formal hedge, there are more suitable plants than bamboo. As informal screening and hedging, they make an elegant light wall of foliage which provides a level of privacy and shelter without being too oppressive.

SUITABLE GRASSES

When grasses are used for edges or hedges, we get the lovely combination of formal and informal. Planting in straight rows or geometric shapes gives the formality, which is immediately contrasted by the soft floppy outlines of the grasses. This mixture of informal and formal is a classic garden trick and is often very effective.

For edging you should choose grasses that are

BAMBOOS FOR SCREENING
- *Chusquea culeou*
- *Fargesia murieliae*
- *Fargesia nitida*
- *Pseudosasa japonica*
- *Semiarundinaria fastuosa*

generally well behaved, and that do not flop too far or spread unduly. If they are evergreen then this is a bonus.

The edging need not be one entire ribbon of the same plant but could be mixed. For example, golden Hakone grass (*Hakonechloa macra* 'Aureola') used with lady's mantle (*Alchemilla mollis*) makes a lovely soft lemon-yellow border with the round green leaves contrasting with the golden grass foliage. Another striking combination is black *Ophiopogon planiscapus* 'Nigrescens' with the variegated sweet flag (*Acorus gramineus* 'Ogon').

Generally, grasses do not really make very practical screens or hedges as many are deciduous and not particularly dense. They would, however, be fast growing and relatively cheap.

Below Coloured leaved sedges such as these make excellent edging plants with colour throughout the year.

EDGING GRASSES
- *Calamogrostis acutiflora* 'Overdam'
- *Carex oshimensis* 'Evergold'
- *Festuca glauca*
- *Hakonechloa macra* 'Aureola'
- *Luzula sylvatica* 'Aurea'
- *Uncinia uncinata* 'Rubra'

TALLER GRASSES FOR HEDGES
- *Arundo donax*
- *Calamagrostis x acutiflora* 'Karl Foerster'
- *Cortaderia selloana*
- *Leymus arenarius*
- *Miscanthus floridulus*
- *Miscanthus sacchariflorus*
- *Miscanthus sinensis* 'Gracillimus'
- *Panicum virgatum*

Roof Gardens

Grasses and bamboos are excellent plants for roof gardens because they are so rarely damaged by wind. Most are so flexible that, however exposed the situation may be, they will usually survive unscathed. If they are damaged by excessively high or cold winds, grasses regrow each year and bamboos produce new leaves afresh each spring so little is lost.

One of the biggest issues with roof gardens is the need to keep the weight of containers and soil to a minimum. Even here, grasses and bamboos are co-operative as they will both grow in shallow and light soils, grasses particularly so. The lightest growing medium for use in a situation such as this would be the soil-less potting composts. These are based on peat, bark, sand or other materials such as coco fibre. Watering will need to be carefully monitored as these composts tend to dry out quite quickly and are difficult to re-wet once dry. Tall plants may be a problem in windy situations in a light compost as they will be prone to blow over. Permanently fixing pots to the surface may be necessary.

Below A modern roof garden with bamboos thriving amongst other screening plants in large raised borders.

Modern Minimal

Minimalist landscapes are currently very fashionable. They can be formal or informal in design, with an emphasis on hard landscaping features like paving, outdoor structures and sculpture. When plants are incorporated, they are few in number, but stunning in appearance. Ornamental grasses and bamboos fit perfectly into this role.

Minimalist gardens usually have very clear lines and geometric patterns. There will be strong vertical and horizontal shapes that are broken only by occasional planting or other features. So a sweep of gravel may be punctuated by a group of upright grasses such as switch grass (*Panicum virgatum*). A sheet of still water in a pool will be the setting for a large clump of the lesser bulrush (*Typha angustifolia*) with its dominant brown flower-heads standing sentinel.

PLANTS FOR MODERN MINIMAL STYLE	
• *Buxus sempervirens*	• *Phormium tenax*
• *Miscanthus sacchariflorus*	• *Phyllostachys nigra*
• *Miscanthus sinensis* 'Gracillimus'	• *Stipa gigantea*
• *Ophiopogon planiscapus* 'Nigrescens'	• *Stipa tenuissima*
	• *Yucca flaccida* 'Ivory'
	• *Zantedeschia aethiopica* 'Crowborough'

MINIMALIST MATERIALS

Construction may be from materials that we will not normally use in the garden. For example, a large wall of mirror may be used to reflect a stand of black bamboo (*Phyllostachys nigra*) growing among black stone chippings. The effect is very simple and the lower side shoots of the bamboo may be removed to reveal the stark black stems.

As well as stone and wood, minimalist gardens will use quite harsh materials such as metal, glass and plastic to make bold statements. The use of light and shade will also be important and such gardens may well come alive at night with the use of artificial lighting.

MINIMALIST STYLE

The atmosphere in these gardens can be very quiet, peaceful and contemplative to many although, like modern art, they may not be attractive to all. Some people may find them cold and harsh.

Plants used in gardens such as these will need to be nearly perfect as each one has to fulfill a particular function. In many situations they will be acting as specimen plants and have to stand on their own. Some of the choicer bamboos such as the golden-stemmed *Phyllostachys vivax* 'Aureocaulis' can be seen at their best in a minimal setting. Colour will often be minimal too, so plain green-leaved grasses are probably most suitable.

Left These blue fescues (*Festuca glauca*) are almost inverted cones in their outline and co-exist strikingly alongside the stone pyramids.

Groundcover Plantings

Some grasses and bamboos are noted for being thugs, invading where they are not wanted and never taking 'No' for an answer. However, in some situations these grasses can be great allies. Sometimes you will want a plant that will rapidly cover inhospitable ground or maybe you have a bank of loose soil that needs stabilizing. In such locations strong-growing invasive grasses can be positively welcomed.

GRASSES FOR GROUNDCOVER

- *Equisetum hyemale* (needs damp soil)
- *Helictotrichon sempervirens*
- *Leymus arenarius*
- *Luzula sylvatica*
- *Phalaris arundinacea* 'Picta'
- *Pleioblastus auricomus*
- *Sasa veitchii*

Left Vigorous grasses and other plants thrive together providing total groundcover, preventing the majority of weed emergence.

Tender Grasses

Some grasses are tender and cannot be grown outside in the garden all year round, but that is not to say they are not worth pursuing. Two such plants are often grown as pot plants. *Oplismenus africanus* 'Variegatus' has green and white variegated leaves with a pink hint, while *Stenotaphrum secundatum* 'Variegatum' has cream variegated foliage. Both have a sprawling habit and can be grown in pots for trailing at the edge of a greenhouse bench or a windowsill. You can also plant them in hanging baskets. Both bear a similarity to wandering Jew (*Tradescantia*) and are often mistaken for them. They need to be grown at around 13°C (55°F). As they get straggly and untidy quite quickly, propagate them frequently by cuttings.

Another tender grass is *Arundo donax versicolor*. This is a tall, striking, variegated grass with broad white-striped leaves, looking very much like a bamboo. It makes a very effective specimen plant in a conservatory and will in time make a large clump. It does not need high temperatures but must not be allowed to freeze in winter. There is also a tender sedge, *Carex phyllocephala* 'Sparkler'. This stunning little plant has green and white variegated leaves like small star-bursts but it must have frost protection over winter.

When grown under glass, grasses may be prone to red spider mite attack which makes the leaves go yellow or brown. A commercial pesticide may be needed in cases of severe attack, but attacks can be successfully prevented by keeping the atmosphere humid around the plants at all times.

Left Here in this tropical garden, *Stenotaphrum secundum* 'Variegatum' grows alongside a purple-leaved tradescantia, providing a colourful contrast.

Materials to Accompany Grasses

Grasses and bamboos are undoubtedly graphic plants. As such they can be used in quite innovative ways and linked to almost any materials in the garden. Their open and ethereal nature contrasts superbly with solid materials such as rock, and simple but very effective schemes can be made from rock, gravel and grasses or bamboos. Gravel and other hard landscape materials seem to act as the best foil for grasses and bamboos. A lawn just doesn't have enough contrast to set off a scheme of ornamental grasses, although it might just work with bamboos.

Grasses and bamboos seem to have a contemporary feel to them and associate well with modern materials such as stainless steel containers, glazed pots, sculpture, painted timberwork screens and decking. By contrast they seem also to work well in a very traditional setting and some effective schemes can be created using items of architectural salvage such as old ironwork, chimney pots or stonework. The trick is to experiment.

Below Sculptures are expensive, but stones, pots, beach-combings and other bric-a-brac can all be used alongside grasses.

6 | A GALLERY OF GRASSESS AND BAMBOOS

Right Large potted specimen grasses such as these make bold statements and can be moved around to give infinite variety.

A–Z Listing

Throughout this book, both common names and botanical names have been used. Many readers may think that common names are easier to use but they are not precise. Many plants have a number of common names and these may vary from country to country, but botanic names are unique and standardized. Therefore whenever you need to be precise about a plant you must use its botanic name. It is the only way to make sure you get exactly the plant you want when purchasing from nurseries and garden centres.

Botanic names are usually divided up into two or three parts. The first word is the genus and the second word is the species. All plants have two names, and many garden plants will have a third name which is called the cultivar. We can take the example *Phalaris arundinacea* 'Feesey'. *Phalaris* is the genus. It is a group name and there are many different types within the genus. The species is *arundinacea*, the form that occurs naturally in the wild. This word actually means 'reed-like' so it tells us a bit about the plant. At some stage someone has either bred or selected a particularly good form of this plant and given it the cultivar name 'Feesey'. This is a unique name.

AGM

The term AGM means Award of Garden Merit, an award given by the Royal Horticultural Society in the United Kingdom. These awards are only given to plants of considerable merit. Catalogues will usually mark these plants with AGM after the name or a little cup symbol. ♉

HARDINESS ZONES

The zone references refer to a hardiness system developed in the USA based on annual minimum temperatures for certain areas. Plants are rated with the lowest zone in which they are likely to survive. See pages 92–93 for the zones and map.

HEIGHTS

Grasses and bamboos will grow successfully in many climates. However, in their native habitats most will achieve greater heights than when they are grown in temperate regions. The heights listed are those that are likely in temperate climates.

***Acorus calamus* 'Variegatus'** (variegated sweet flag) Not a true grass but an aquatic perennial with strap-shaped leaves, longitudinally striped in cream. Grows in shallow water as a marginal. Insignificant flowers. Height: 60–90cm (24–36in). Zone 7.

***Acorus gramineus* 'Hakuro-nishiki'** (Japanese sweet flag) A petite grass-like plant with bright golden yellow variegations and green flashes. Ideal for containers or even a hanging basket. Height: 15cm (6in). Zone 9.

A.g. 'Ogon' Golden yellow, cream and green leaves in a stunning combination. Evergreen and always looks good. Height: 45cm (18in). Zone 7.

A.g. 'Variegatus' Simple green and white variegation but evergreen and very tough. Height: 45cm (18in). Zone 6.

Agrostis nebulosa (cloud bent grass) This is an annual grass producing huge fluffy flowerheads like billowing clouds. Easy to grow. Height: 30cm (12in). Zone 7.

Alopecurus pratensis 'Aureovariegatus'

***Alopecurus pratensis* 'Aureovariegatus'** (golden foxtail grass) A charming small stubby grass with leaves striped in yellow and green. Height: 30cm (12in). Zone 4.

***Arrhenatherum elatius bulbosum* 'Variegatum'** (bulbous oat grass) A long name for a diminutive plant! A tufted herbaceous perennial with grey-green leaves edged in white, and conspicuous brown flowers in summer. The bases of

Arundo donax 'Variegata'

the stems are swollen like small bulbs. Height: 20cm (8in). Zone 6.

Arundo donax (giant reed) A tall herbaceous perennial which can remain evergreen in mild winters. The huge, arching green leaves are borne on fat stems. Makes a superb specimen plant. Prefers a moist site and is borderline hardy. Does not need cutting down if the foliage remains green. Height: 3.6m (12ft). Zone 7.

A.d. versicolor Similar to the above but with strikingly variegated foliage. Excellent in an exotic sub-tropical scheme. Not so vigorous and definitely tender so it must be overwintered in a frost-free place. Well worth the extra effort it requires. Older plants can be quite stupendous. Height: 3m (10ft). Zone 8.

Bouteloua gracilis (blue grama grass) Short clumps of narrow green leaves which turn purplish and then tan in the autumn. Flowers are silvery pink, clustered in little combs on top of slender stems. Likes full sun and a well-drained, warm site. Height: 45cm (18in). Zone 5.

Briza maxima (greater quaking grass) Vigorous hardy annual grass grown primarily for its pendulous purple and green locket-shaped flowers. Good for drying. Height: 45cm (18in). Zone 5.

Bromus inermis **'Skinner's Gold'** (brome) A vigorous grass with masses of golden yellow stems with yellow and green stripy foliage. Lofty panicles of creamy flowers appear throughout the summer. Quite striking. Likes full sun and moist, well-drained soil. Inclined to be invasive. Height: 60cm (24in). Zone 7.

Calamagrostis x *acutiflora* **'Karl Foerster'** (feather reed grass) Makes tight tussocks of thin mid-green leaves topped with wiry flowering stems of feathery soft orange flower-heads with a touch of purple. The flowers remain into winter and it does not self-seed. Height: 1.8m (6ft). Zone 4.
C.a. **'Overdam'** Impressive mounds of green and white stripy leaves setting off the pinkish feathery flower plumes. Needs a sunny open spot. Height: 90cm (36in). Zone 4.

Carex buchananii (red fox sedge) Extremely narrow foliage with an erect habit. Reddish brown foliage and a prominent flower spike. Height: 45cm (18in). Zone 7.

Carex comans 'Bronze Form' (New Zealand hair sedge) This has dense tufts of narrow deep bronze leaves. Height: 15cm (6in). Zone 7.
Carex **'Frosted Curls'** Thin, curling silvery green foliage with a pendant habit. Height: 45cm (18in). Zone 7.
Carex elata **'Aurea'** (Bowles' golden sedge) Wonderful golden green grass-like foliage with darker edges. Good by moist water margins. Evergreen. Height: 45cm (18in). Zone 7.
Carex morrowii **'Variegata'** Brilliant white variegated sedge, very compact and easy to grow. Likes a damp shady site. Height: 60cm (24in). Zone 8.
Carex oshimensis **'Evergold'** AGM A dense tussock with luminous gold variegated foliage. A splendid form. Height: 30cm (12in). Zone 5.
Carex pendula (great drooping sedge) Tufted evergreen perennial preferring moist or wet soil. The arching stems bear weeping catkin-like dark brown flower spikes. Height: 1.2m (4ft). Zone 8.
Carex phyllocephala **'Sparkler'** This is a stunning little sedge, although being tender it must be grown with protection in many areas. It produces whorls of pointed leaves edged in white with touches of pink. Dark brown flower spikes. It grows best in shade. Height: 45cm (17¾in). Zone 8.

Chasmanthium latifolium (wild oats, Northern sea oats) A woodland grass grown mainly for its stiffly trailing flowers. The flattened spikelets start out olive green and mature to a well-tanned bronze for winter. Flowers late summer. Height: 1m (3ft). Zone 6.

Calamagrostis x *acutiflora* **'Overdam'**

Chimonobambusa marmorea A handsome bamboo with slender lime-green culms which mature to purple-green. Height: 1.5m (5ft). Zone 6.

Chionochloa conspicua (snow grass, tussock grass) This makes a bold green tussock, bearing exquisite feathery plumes. It likes a warm sunny position. Height: 1.5m (5ft). Zone 7.

Chusquea culeou AGM (Chilean bamboo, foxtail bamboo) A tall bamboo with thick solid canes. An abundance of small leaves is produced on many fine branches, giving an almost shuttlecock-like effect. Newly emerging canes look like asparagus tips. Very hardy and wind resistant. Height: 3.6–4m (12–13ft). Zone 7.

Chusquea culeou

Coix lacryma-jobi (Job's tears) This is a half-hardy annual grass with broad light green foliage. Grown for the attractive bead-like seeds which turn a greyish-mauve on ripening. Height: 45cm (18in). Zone 9.

Cortaderia fulvida (toe-toe grass) Large mound-forming species. Broad arching green leaves are topped with soaring slender stems bearing large, loose and lopsided plumes of dusky pink flowers. Sadly it can be disappointing in temperate climates. Needs damp soil, preferably near water. Height: 2.4m (8ft). Zone 8.

Cortaderia richardii

Cortaderia richardii (New Zealand pampas grass) A graceful pampas producing fine foliage and smaller elegant drooping plumes in early summer. Well worth growing. Suitable for the smaller garden as it is not so bulky. Height: 2.1m (7ft). Zone 8.

Cortaderia selloana (pampas grass) This is one of the best-known and most vigorous of ornamental grasses. The foliage alone makes a splendid statement throughout much of the year but in autumn it comes into its own when it produces towering creamy plumes. It is evergreen so even in winter it has some value. Height: 2.1m (7ft). Zone 5.

C.s. 'Aureolineata' AGM (syn. 'Gold Band') This plant has everything that the species has but the leaves are variegated golden yellow. There is also a similar silver-variegated type called 'Silver Stripe'. Both are very useful plants in many situations, looking good for most of the year. Height: 1.5m (5ft). Zone 5.

C.s. 'Pumila' AGM (dwarf pampas grass) An excellent compact form of pampas with typical flowerheads on shorter plants. Height: 1.5m (5ft). Zone 5.

C.s. 'Rendatleri' (pink pampas) Similar to the species but with looser pink spikes. Inclined to be brittle and break in the wind. Height: 2.1m (7ft). Zone 5.

C.s. 'Sunningdale Silver' AGM (silver pampas grass) This is a selected version of the species with spectacular plumes. Height: 2.1m (7ft). Zone 5.

Cymbopogon citratus (lemon grass) A tropical grass highly prized for its use in cookery. Perennial but can be grown from seed. Height: 1.5m (5ft). Zone 9.

Cyperus longus (galingale) Loose clumps of elegant green foliage with brownish flowers. Grows in marshy places by streams and pools. Sun or shade. Height: 90cm (36in). Zone 7.

Cyperus papyrus (papyrus) A very showy exotic that in warm summers can make a lofty plant in a season. The slender vivid green stems are topped by the typical shaggy mop-heads composed of hundreds of green thread-like bracts. Not hardy in temperate climates so must be treated as a summer plant and overwintered under protection. Height: 2.1m (7ft). Zone 9.

Deschampsia cespitosa (tufted hair grass) With its delicate sprays of cloud-like flowers and delicate foliage, this is a distinctive grass in both flower and foliage. It grows best in damp soils and tolerates shade. Height: 1.2m (4ft). Zone 4. There are many good forms such as **'Bronzeschleier'** (syn 'Bronze Veil') with brown flowers. Long lasting effect. Also **'Goldtau'** (syn 'Golden Dew') which is more compact with silvery spikelets that age to golden yellow. Height: 75cm (30in). Zone 4.

Deschampsia cespitosa 'Goldtau'

Deschampsia flexuosa (wavy hair grass) Similar to the above but smaller in all appearances. Grows in dry shade. **'Tatra Gold'** has gaudy yellowish foliage and showy red-brown flowers. Height: 60cm (24in). Zone 4.

Equisetum hyemale (scouring rush, horsetail) Grown for its clumps of bright green stems. The leaves are reduced to small scales that appear as cream and brown bands. A marginal plant that likes up to 10cm (4in) of water over its roots. Like most horsetails, it is vigorous and spreads. Best grown in containers to avoid problems of invasion. Height: 60cm (24in). Zone 7.

Fargesia murieliae AGM (Muriel's bamboo) Originally collected in 1913 from China by Ernest Wilson who named it after his daughter Muriel. An elegant and easy bamboo with tall, thin, gently swaying canes and masses of small green leaves. The canes are green at first, maturing to a dull yellow. Clump forming and well behaved. Height: 2.4–3.6m (8–12ft). Zone 5. Various cultivars are available such as **'Harewood'**, a dwarf cultivar growing to 90cm (36in), and **'Jumbo'**, a vigorous, very hardy clone with broad leaves growing to 4m (13ft). **'Simba' AGM** is another compact grower which forms clumps up to 1.8 (6ft).

Fargesia nitida AGM Very similar to *F. murieliae* but with more upright canes with a purplish hue from the second year. Clump forming. Height: 4m (13ft). Zone 4. **'Nymphenburg' AGM** is much more compact with a graceful weeping habit and longer, narrower leaves.

Festuca glauca (blue fescue) Forms a tight globe of narrow glaucous foliage and associates beautifully with many plants. A good tough non-invasive groundcover. Easily grown from seed. **'Elijah Blue'** is a deeper darker blue and is becoming widely available. **'Golden Toupee'** is a curious combination of yellowish green but

Festuca glauca 'Golden Toupee'

with underlying blue in the centre of the crown. Height: 15cm (6in). Zone 5.

***Glyceria maxima* 'Variegata'** (variegated manna grass) A grass that revels in moist soil conditions and will thrive at the edge of a pool as a marginal plant in up to 15cm (6in) of water. The sturdy strap-like leaves are variegated with cream and tinted with pink in summer. In water, grow in a basket to restrict spread. Height: 90cm (36in). Zone 5.

Hakonechloa macra (Hakone grass) Forms a loose mound of glossy leaves that turn copper in autumn. Airy greenish to tan panicles in late summer. Grow in partial shade, or sun if the soil is moist. Height: 45cm (18in). Zone 5.

H.m. **'Aureola' AGM** One of the finest of the striped grasses with golden foliage turning bronze in late summer. The clump slowly spreads. Mature plants look lovely in a permanent container where the fullness of the foliage will spread and soften the container. Attractive red-brown summer flowers. Dies back in winter but still well worth growing. Likes a moist soil. Height: 20cm (8in). Zone 5.

***Helictotrichon sempervirens* AGM** (blue oat grass) This grass makes an architectural statement, with blue foliage and remarkable oat-like flowers held high above the foliage. A 'must have'. Useful as a small specimen or associated with other plants in a border. Height: 90cm (36in). Zone 4.

x *Hibanobambusa tranquillans* 'Shiroshima' AGM A naturally occurring hybrid bamboo. Active habit but easily controlled. One of the best variegated bamboos with large, glossy green leaves with creamy variegations. The culms are grooved on one side. Tolerant of dry conditions. Height: 2.1–3m (7–10ft). Zone 8.

Hordeum jubatum (foxtail barley) A tufted hardy annual grown for its decorative barley-like flower spikes. Useful as a filler in a mixed border but beware as it seeds freely. Height: 45cm (18in). Zone 5.

***Imperata cylindrica* 'Rubra'** (Japanese blood grass) Probably the most opulent of all grasses, famed for its blood-red foliage. The young foliage emerges green in spring with just a tinge of red at the tips, but as the season progresses the red suffuses down the entire leaves. A few leaves remain green, giving a startling contrast. Likes moist fertile soil in the sun. It spreads slowly. Height: 30cm (12in). Zone 7.

Hakonechloa macra 'Aureola'

x *Hibanobambusa tranquillans* 'Shiroshima'

Indocalamus solidus (solid stem bamboo) Broad dark green leaves on slender culms. Excellent groundcover. Active but easily controlled. Shade tolerant. Height: 1.2m (4ft). Zone 6.
Indocalamus tessellatus Tall culms are bowed low by a heavy clothing of large green leaves. Leaves can be as much as 60cm (24in) long by 10cm (4in) wide. Gives a sub-tropical effect. Slender green culms have a waxy bloom. Makes a mound shape and often appears short due to weeping habit. Active but easily controlled. Height: 1.8m (6ft). Zone 5.

Isolepis cernua A close tufted plant with very fine green leaves, sometimes called the optic fibre plant. Usually grown in pots or unusual containers for its quirky appearance. Height: 15cm (6in). Zone 8.

***Juncus effusus* 'Spiralis'** (corkscrew rush) This plant forms clumps of curiously twisted and curled green leafless stems. Curious rather than beautiful! Needs full sun or light shade and moist soil. Height: 45cm (18in). Zone 4.

Koeleria glauca (blue hair grass) Silvery, blue-green foliage with attractive cream and green flower heads. Like a broader-leaved *Festuca glauca*. Height: 20cm (8in). Zone 4.

Lagurus ovatus

Lagurus ovatus AGM (hare's tail)
A hardy annual grass producing masses of soft greenish tufty heads fading to white. Good for drying. Height: 30cm (12in). Zone 9.

Leymus arenarius (blue lyme grass)
This vigorous grass has intense blue foliage that can look quite striking in plant combinations. It is however rampant and invasive. Excellent for stabilizing loose banks and colonizing difficult sites. Height: 90cm (36in). Zone 4.

Luzula sylvatica (greater woodrush)
An excellent groundcover for dry shady places. The large tussocks of evergreen leaves spread slowly. Small brown flowerheads are held above the foliage. 'Aurea' has yellow foliage which deepens throughout the winter to a rich burnished gold in cold weather. Height: 45cm (18in). Zone 6.

Milium effusum 'Aureum' AGM
(Bowle's golden grass, golden wood millet) This short-lived perennial acts like an annual and seeds frequently. The golden yellow foliage is soft and pleasantly ragged with insignificant yellow flowers. It tolerates full sun but prefers light shade and a moist site. Height: 30cm (12in). Zone 6.

Miscanthus floridulus AGM (giant miscanthus) Huge clumps of long arching green leaves, turning reddish or purplish in the autumn then tan for the winter. The silvery flower tassels are tinted with pale lavender. May not bloom in cool or short season areas. Full sun and well-drained fertile soil. Height: 3.3m (11ft). Zone 4.
Miscanthus sacchariflorus (silver banner grass, amur grass) An enormous species but not fully hardy. The broad arching leaves make it useful as a screen or background plant. It spreads slowly and may be disappointing in cool climates. Height: 3m (10ft). Zone 7.
Miscanthus sinensis 'Cabaret' Thick ribbon-like leaves with bold milky-white linear centres and dark green leaf margins. Lofty foliage is topped with copper flowers in early autumn. The flower stems blush pink and the seedheads fluff to a creamy colour with age. 'Cosmopolitan' AGM is very similar but perhaps not so spectacular with central and marginal leaf stripes. Height: 1.8m (6ft). Zone 7.
  M.s. 'Goldfeder' A distinctive variegated grass with broad leaves boldly striped with gold, green and white. Open loose habit with creamy flowers held well above the foliage. Height: 2.1m (7ft). Zone 6.
  M.s. 'Gracillimus' (maiden grass) A clump-forming grass with narrow dark green leaves followed by sprays of white flowers, although these are not reliably produced. A valuable contrast to other more highly coloured plants. Height: 45cm (18in). Zone 5.
  M.s. 'Kleine Fontäne' Upright mounds of thin green foliage with many delicate pink flowers fading to a creamy colour. Height: 1.5m (5ft). Zone 5.
  M.s. 'Malepartus' A striking upright plant with broad leaves, bearing a single central white band. Copious heads of creamy white flowers, becoming very fluffy and white when dry. Height: 1.8m (6ft). Zone 7.
  M.s. 'Morning Light' AGM
A choice cultivar noted for its very narrow green leaves with white variegation on the margins. The foliage

has an overall silvery appearance and forms upright, rounded clumps. The leaves eventually turn straw-beige by winter. Tiny reddish-copper flowers appear in long tassel-like inflorescences above the foliage, gradually turning into silvery white plumes as the seeds mature. Blooms later than most. The flower plumes persist well into winter, providing good winter interest. Height: 1.5m (5ft) Zone 5.
  M.s. 'Silberfeder' The name (silver feather) refers to the large feathery flowers that emerge silver with only the barest hint of pink. The plant has a quite a lax habit and often flops, but does so gracefully and makes a loose mound. Free flowering. Height: 1.8m (6ft). Zone 7.
  M.s. 'Variegatus' Probably the most widely grown of the coloured-leaved miscanthus with creamy white and pale green longitudinal stripes. Height: 1.5m (5ft). Zone 6.

Miscanthus sinensis 'Variegatus'

  M.s. 'Zebrinus' AGM (zebra grass) A very popular cultivar with green leaves conspicuously banded with gold. A loose-growing, clump-forming perennial. Some sprays of white flowers appear in the autumn but the plant is prized for its foliage. Height: 1.2m (4ft). Zone 6.

Molinia caerulea (purple moor grass) A densely tufted perennial grass which performs to its best in damp soils. Flower spikes are a subtle purple but small and indistinct. The foliage turns yellow in autumn. Totally deciduous, naturally shedding its stems in early winter. Slow to establish, so buy a large plant. Height: 90cm (36in). Zone 5.

M.c. arundinacea Taller version of the species, most often seen as cultivars such as '**Skyracer**' (2.1m/7ft) or '**Karl Foerster**' (1.5m/5ft). Zone 5.

M.c. '**Variegata**' AGM The leaves are striped light yellow to creamy white. It is worth growing for its foliage alone but flowering can also be spectacular. Height: 90cm (36in). Zone 5.

Molinia caerulea 'Variegata'

Oplismenus africanus '**Variegatus**' AGM This jolly little grass masquerades as a tradescantia, making a trailing mound of variegated foliage. What adds to the confusion is that, being tender, it is often grown in pots. Small purple flowers in late summer. Height: 60cm (24in). Zone 9.

Panicum virgatum (switch grass, panic grass) A very variable prairie grass, clump-forming but also runs. Becoming increasingly popular as a garden plant and available as many named cultivars. Height: 1.2–2.1m (4–7ft). Zone 5.

P.v. '**Heavy Metal**' A glaucous blue selection. Very upright. Height: 1.5m (5ft). Zone 5.

P.v. '**Rotstrahlbusch**' One of a number of cultivars that change from green summer foliage to rich red tones. Height: 1.2m (4ft). Zone 5.

Pennisetum alopecuroides (fountain grass) The foliage forms a fountain of narrow arching green leaves, attractive but unassuming. The flowers are its main feature, being large and yellowish with dominant bristles making them look like large hairy caterpillars. Height: 90cm (36in). Zone 6.

P.a. '**Hameln**' is a good cultivar. Height: 60cm (24in). Zone 6.

Pennisetum glaucum '**Purple Majesty**' (purple millet) Tall, dark and handsome describes this purple-leaved millet. Young plants have green leaves, but exposure to direct sunlight stimulates the development of the purple leaf colour. Mature leaves are long and slender, with a red midrib. It is tall and stately with strong flower-heads. The immature spikes can be cut and used in floral arrangements, or left on the plant to attract birds that feed on the seeds. 'Purple Majesty' is very easy to grow and is very tolerant of heat and low moisture. Height: 90cm (36in). Zone 8.

Pennisetum glaucum 'Purple Majesty'

Pennisetum orientale AGM (oriental fountain grass) The greyish green leaves form a small compact clump. Pale pink-mauve fluffy flower spikes like small bottle brushes appear throughout the summer. The delicate effect is lovely with old roses. Needs well-drained soil and full sun. Height: 90cm (36in). Zone 7.

Pennisetum setaceum '**Rubrum**' (purple fountain grass) This is one of the most spectacular of all grasses. This wonderful plant has an upright habit with broad leaves in a rich glowing burgundy. Flowers are produced in late summer, which just happen to be a lovely toning pink. Overall the effect is charming. Widely used in warmer climates as a landscape plant. In temperate areas it must be overwintered under glass and even then may be difficult. Well worth the extra effort though. Height: 60cm (24in). Zone 9.

Pennisetum setaceum 'Rubrum'

Pennisetum villosum (feathertop) Forms waterfalls of beautiful pale green foliage topped with copious quantities of large, furry caterpillar-like flowers in parchment colour. Very effective in groups. Likes a well-drained site in full sun. Height: 60cm (24in). Zone 8.

Phalaris arundinacea '**Picta**' AGM (gardener's garters, reed canary grass, ribbon grass) This is the variegated form as the common green species is rarely grown, being a troublesome and invasive weed in some areas. Even the variegated type grows freely and spreads vigorously. It is nevertheless a cheerful grass with white variegation and can be very useful for stabilizing banks or filling difficult areas where other plants fail to grow. '**Feesey**' is an improved form with a more pronounced variegation and pink flushes in the spring. Height: 90cm (36in). Zone 4.

Phyllostachys aurea AGM (fishpole bamboo, golden bamboo) A tall bamboo with green foliage and grooved green canes fading to gold. The best colourings occur in bright sunlight. The nodes are compressed to give curious knobbly culms. Very upright and leafy so makes an effective screening plant. Drought tolerant. Height: 2.4–3.6m (8–12ft). Zone 6.

   P.a. '**Albovariegata**' has crisply variegated white and green foliage. One of the few tall variegated bamboos. Height: 4m (13ft). Zone 6.

Phyllostachys bambusoides '**Castillonis**' AGM (giant timber bamboo, golden brilliant bamboo) Grown for its golden canes which are thick with distinct green grooves. Leaves are large and lightly variegated. Upright habit and spreads slowly. '**Castillonis Inversa**' has green culms with a yellow groove. Height: 3–4.5m (10–15ft). Zone 7.

Phyllostachys bissetii A vigorous and hardy species making dense thickets of strong dark green culms. Good for shelter or hedging, but can spread. Height: 7m (23ft). Zone 6.

Phyllostachys nigra AGM (black bamboo) The green canes ripen through purple to deep shiny ebony black by the second or third season. Prefers bright sunshine and a warm sheltered site. Slender arching habit and reasonably well behaved. Very popular and readily available. Height: 4m (13ft). Zone 7.

Phyllostachys vivax '**Aureocaulis**' AGM Vigorous, very hardy species with heavy drooping foliage. This cultivar is highly desired for its banana yellow culms with irregular green stripes. Open sunny aspect or light shade. Height:4m (13ft). Zone 8.

Pleioblastus auricomus AGM (gold-leaved bamboo) Delightful compact plant with rich golden evergreen foliage. Velvety to the touch. Needs bright sun and prefers a moist site. Spreading but not over invasive; makes an excellent groundcover plant. Can be cut to the ground each spring for

Pleioblastus auricomus

vigorous colourful regrowth. An excellent tub plant. Height: 1.5m (5ft). Zone 7.

Pleioblastus pygmaeus Another dwarf groundcover bamboo with a tendency to run and be invasive. Grow in a container or use where its exuberance can be beneficial. Small green leaves on slender culms with purplish nodes and tiny bristles. Sun or shade. Height: 30cm (12in). Zone 6.

Pleioblastus shibuyanus '**Tsuboi**' Small leaves pleasingly variegated. Compact but can spread. One of the best variegated bamboos. Height: 1.8m (6ft). Zone 7.

Pleioblastus variegatus AGM A low-growing mound-shaped bamboo with creamy white-striped leaves. Spiky appearance. Useful for groundcover in sun or light shade. 75cm (30in). Zone 7.

Poa chaixii (broad-leaved meadow grass) A woodland grass grown for its shiny green leaves and purplish flowers borne in early summer. Height: 90cm (36in). Zone 5.

Pseudosasa japonica AGM (arrow bamboo) A useful tough species which makes a good windbreak or hedge. Also good as a specimen. Upright habit, arching at the apex with large glossy dark green leaves on olive green canes. Clump-forming so well behaved.

Pseudosasa japonica

Tolerates wet conditions. Rustles nicely in the breeze. Height: 4m (13ft). Zone 6.

Saccharum ravennae (Ravenna grass) A tall grass with arching grey-green foliage which turns reddish-brown in the autumn. Huge purple-tinted silver plumes are produced in late summer and early autumn. A tender species which only performs well with hot summers. Can be disappointing in temperate climates. Height: 3.6m (12ft). Zone 7.

Sasa veitchii (Veitch's bamboo) The thin canes have a purplish hue and are hidden by large boat-shaped green leaves. The leaf tips wither to a dull white paper-like variegation with cold weather, thought by many to be its attractive feature. Very effective as a groundcover plant. Spreads very vigorously so use with care. Sun or shade. Height: 1.5m (5ft). Zone 5.

Schoenoplectus subsp *tabernaemontani* '**Albescens**' (white bulrush) A variegated form of the common bulrush. A clump-forming aquatic plant at home in shallow water. Much less vigorous than the plain species. '**Zebrinus**' (zebra bulrush) is similar but the stripes are across the leaves as horizontal bands. Height: 1.5m (5ft). Zone 5.

***Semiarundinaria fastuosa* AGM** (Narihira bamboo) A stiff, upright, regal bamboo with dull green canes maturing to red-brown in sunshine. The dense foliage makes it a good windbreak or screening plant. Sun or shade. Height: 5m (16½ft). Zone 7.

***Setaria macrostachya* AGM** (fox tail millet) An attractive annual grass with light green leaves. The numerous flowerheads have reddish tints. Dries well for winter decoration. Height: 90cm (36in). Zone 6.

Shibataea kumasasa A charming and well-behaved small bamboo with apple-green foliage. The canes are slender and zigzag in form. Prefers moisture and a warm site. Spreads slowly. Height: 60cm (24in). Zone 6.

***Spartina pectinata* 'Aureomarginata'** (striped prairie cord grass) This is a tall herbaceous perennial which makes a good specimen plant. Foliage is striped with yellow which matures to a soft brown later in the season. Plumes of purplish flowers are produced in late summer. Spreads slowly in a dry soil but much faster in a moist situation. Height: 1.8m (6ft). Zone 5.

***Stenotaphrum secundatum* 'Variegatum' AGM** (St Augustine grass, buffalo grass) A tender perennial grass with variegated leaves. It is small in stature so suitable for growing in pots in a greenhouse in temperate areas. Creeps indefinitely, rooting at the nodes, so in pots it is best to propagate frequently to keep small compact plants. Can also be grown in hanging baskets. Height: 15cm (6in). Zone 10.

Stipa arundinacea (pheasant grass) Mainly grown for its mound of khaki-green foliage which turns orange brown in late summer. Colours best on poor soils. Sprays of greenish-purple flowers are borne in late summer. Height: 90cm (36in). Zone 8.

***Stipa gigantea* AGM** (golden oats, Spanish oat grass) Another fine

Stipa gigantea

perennial grass which makes an outstanding specimen plant. Foliage is a tight clump of grey-green leaves, topped with huge wide open heads of glittering bronze and gilt oat-like flowers. These are produced in mid-summer but last well into winter. Height: 2.4m (8ft). Zone 8.

Stipa tenuissima (pony tail grass) A short-leaved perennial with hair-like bright emerald green leaves. Produces feathery brown flowers in mid-summer. Delicate waterfall habit. Being so light, it billows with every breath of wind. Seeds freely and seems to breed true. Height: 75cm (30in). Zone 7.

***Thamnocalamus crassinodus* 'Kew Beauty'** An upright-growing bamboo with tiny leaves, arching with age. Young culms are covered with a blue-silver bloom, aging reddish. Makes a good specimen. Prefers light shade. Height: 4m (13ft). Zone 7.

Typha angustifolia (lesser bulrush, narrow-leaved reed mace, soft flag) A less rampant version of the common bulrush. Dark brown sausage-like flowers top the slender green foliage. A deep marginal plant for larger pools and water features. Height: 2.1m (7ft). Zone 4.

***Uncinia uncinata* rubra** (red hook sedge) The rich mahogany red foliage makes this a distinct plant. Erect habit and bonus of being evergreen. Very useful in winter bedding and containers. Prefers full sun and moist soil. Height: 30cm (12in). Zone 7.

***Yushania anceps* AGM** Beautiful but rampant species of bamboo. The shiny green culms are covered with white bloom. Abundant mid-green foliage. Useful as a screen. Height: 3–3.6m (10–12ft). Zone 6.

***Zea mays* 'Variegata'** (striped corn, variegated corn) These are cultivated forms of the annual fodder crop maize or garden vegetable sweetcorn. Seed merchants offer various types such as **'Quadricolor'** or **'Harlequin'**. These are grown for their broad leaves striped with white, green, pink or red. They are tall and strong growing and often used as statements in bedding displays or exotic plantings. Forms such as **'Strawberry Corn'** or **'Fiesta'** are grown for their coloured cobs which can be dried for indoor winter display. All are tender and need to be grown from seed sown in warm conditions in late spring. Height: 2.4m (8ft). Zone 7.

Zea mays '**Variegata**'

Hardiness Zones

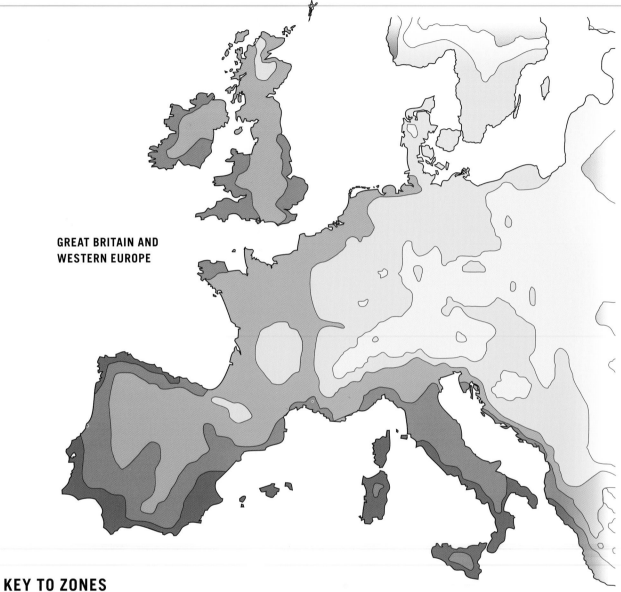

**GREAT BRITAIN AND
WESTERN EUROPE**

KEY TO ZONES

ZONE	CELSIUS	FAHRENHEIT
Zone 1	below -46°C	(below -50°F)
Zone 2	-46 to -40°C	(-50 to -40°F)
Zone 3	-40 to -34°C	(-40 to -30°F)
Zone 4	-34 to -29°C	(-30 to -20°F)
Zone 5	-29 to -23°C	(-20 to -10°F)
Zone 6	-23 to -18°C	(-10 to 0°F)
Zone 7	-18 to -12°C	(0 to 10°F)
Zone 8	-12 to -7°C	(10 to 20°F)
Zone 9	-7 to -1°C	(20 to 30°F)
Zone 10	-1 to 4°C	(30 to 40°F)
Zone 11	above 4°C	(above 40°F)

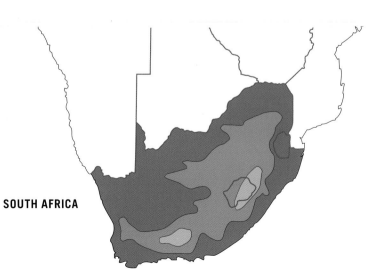

SOUTH AFRICA

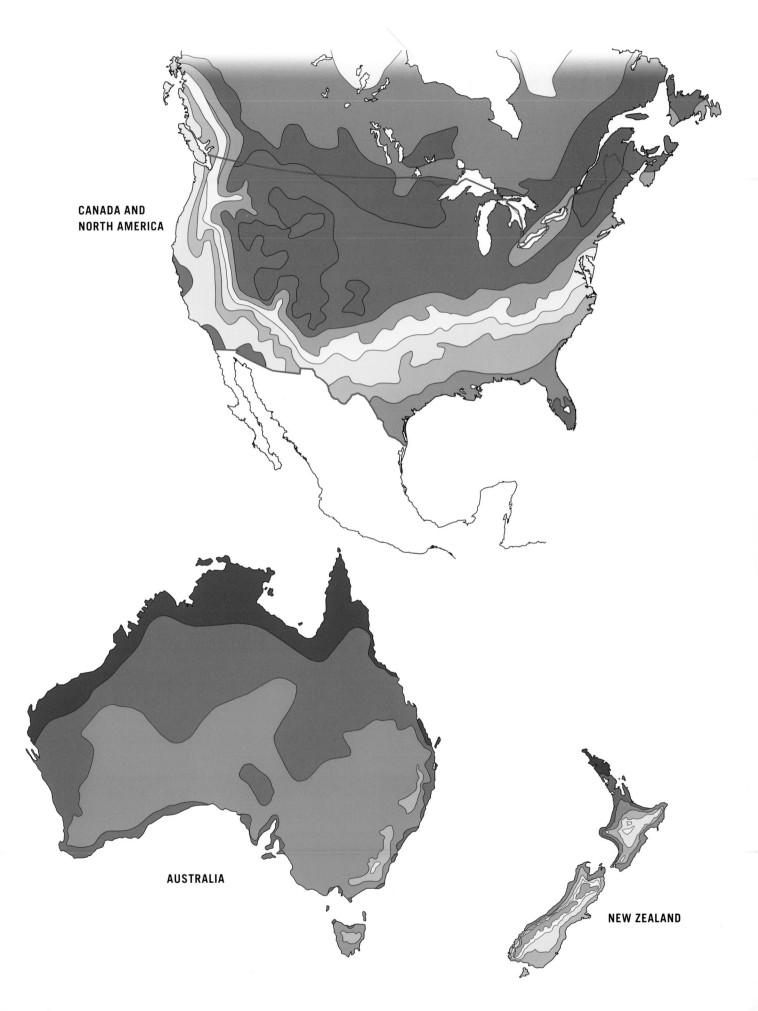

CANADA AND
NORTH AMERICA

AUSTRALIA

NEW ZEALAND

Suppliers

UK

Apple Court Nurseries
Hordle Lane
Hordle
Lymington
Hampshire SO41 0HU
Tel: 01590 642130
Email: applecourt@btinternet.com
www.applecourt.com
Wide range of grasses, hostas, ferns and other herbaceous plants.

The Beth Chatto Gardens Ltd
Elmstead Market
Colchester
Essex CO7 7DB
Tel: 01206 822007
Email: info@bethchatto.fsnet.co.uk
www.bethchatto.co.uk
Wide range of unusual plants, mainly herbaceous, including a good range of grasses.

The Big Grass Company
Hookhill Plantation
Woolfardisworthy East
Near Crediton
Devon EX17 4RX
Tel: 01363 866146
Email: alison@big-grass-co.co.uk
www.big-grass.com
Wonderful range of grasses, sedges, rushes, bamboos and restios.

Drysdale Garden Exotics
Bowerwood Road
Fordingbridge
Hampshire SP6 1BN
Tel: 01425 653010
Bamboos and plants for exotic and Mediterranean gardens.

Four Seasons Perennials
Forncett St Mary
Norwich
Norfolk NR16 1JT
Tel: 01508 488344
Email: contact@fsperennials.co.uk.
www.fsperennials.co.uk
Very wide range of hardy perennials, including many grasses.

Hoecroft Plants
Severals Grange
Holt Road
Wood Norton
Dereham
Norfolk NR20 5BL
Tel: 01362 684206
Email: hoecroft@acedial.co.uk
www.hoecroft.co.uk
Ornamental grasses and herbaceous perennials with the emphasis on coloured and variegated leaves.

Jungle Giants
Burford House Gardens
Tenbury Wells
Worcestershire WR15 8HQ
Tel: 01584 819885
Email: bamboo@junglegiants.co.uk
www.junglegiants.co.uk
Bamboo specialists.

Knoll Gardens
Hampreston
Wimborne
Dorset BH21 7ND
Tel: 01202 873931
Email: enquiries@knollgardens.co.uk
www.knollgardens.co.uk
Wide range of grasses including many new and unusual types. Also herbaceous perennials.

Mozart House Nursery
84 Central Avenue
Wigston Magna
Wigston
Leicestershire LE18 2AA
Telephone: 0116 288 9548
Specializes in bamboos but also supplies ornamental grasses and ferns.

Mulu Nurseries
Longdon Hill
Wickhamford
Evesham
Worcestershire WR11 7RP
Tel: 01386 833171
Email: sales@mulu.co.uk
www.mulu.co.uk
Wide range of exotic plants including bamboos, restios and a few grasses.

The Ornamental Grass and Plant Nursery
Church Farm
Westgate
Rillington
Malton
N. Yorkshire YO17 8LN
Tel: 01944 758247
Email: sales@ornamentalgrass.co.uk
www.ornamentalgrass.co.uk
Mainly grasses but also some bamboos, ferns and hostas.

AUSTRALIA

NEW SOUTH WALES

Bamboo World
1053 Teven Road
Tuckombil NSW 2477
Tel: (02) 6628 6988
www.bambooworld.com.au

Mr Bamboo
18 Myoora Road
Terrey Hills NSW 2084
Tel: (02) 9486 3604

Native & Ornamental Grasses, Wetlands & Turf
Lot 3 Cupitts Lane
Clarendon NSW 2756
Tel: (612) 4577 5912
Fax: (612) 4577 5736
Email: info@abulk.com.au

QUEENSLAND

Bamboo Australia Pty. Ltd.
1171 Kenilworth Road
Belli Park QLD 4562
Tel: (07) 5447 0299

SOUTH AUSTRALIA

S Heading Bamboo Products
PO Box 303
Adelaide SA 5001
Tel: (08) 8338 4101

WESTERN AUSTRALIA

Western Bamboo
Leeming WA 6149
Tel: (08) 9575 7507

NEW ZEALAND

Bamboo Specialists
833 West Coast Road
Oratia
Tel: (09) 814 9847
(mobile) 021 1620846
www.bamboogro@xtra.co.nz

Oratia Native Plant Nursery
625 West Coast Road
Oratia
Tel: (09) 818 6467
www.oratianatives.co.nz

Palmers
• Browns Bay
  26-28 Anzac Road
  Tel: (09) 479 4558
• Glen Eden
  Gt North Road
  Tel: (09) 818 7159
• Glenfield
  129 Diana Drive
  Tel: (09) 444 6077
• Hobsonville
  cnr Hobsonville & Brigham
  Creek Roads
  Tel: (09) 416 8110
• Newmarket
  73 Remuera Road
  Tel: (09) 529 2192
• Papuranga
  cnr Pigeon Mountain &
  Papuranga Roads
  Tel: (09) 534 6847
• Remuera
  cnr Shore & Orakei Roads
  Tel: (09) 524 4037
• Takanini
  226 Gt South Road
  Takanini
  Tel: (09) 298 7622

Plantarama
• Westgate
  104 Highway 16
  Massey
  Tel: (09) 416 7707
• Papakura
  524 Gt South Road
  Tel: (09) 298 1494
  www.plantarama.co.nz

Roger Hunters' Garden Centre
39 Tidal Road
Mangere East
Tel: (09) 275 4209

SOUTH AFRICA

WESTERN CAPE

Starke Ayres Garden Centre
21 Liesbeek Parkway
Rosebank, 7700
Tel: (021) 685 4120
Fax: (021) 685 3837
Email: starkeayres@iafrica.com or
sandy@thegardencentre.co.za
www.thegardencentre.co.za

Stodels
• Eversdal Road
  Bellville
  Tel: (021) 919 1107
  Fax: (021) 919 9324
  mail@stodels.com
• Doncaster Road
  Kenilworth, 7700
  Tel: (021) 671 9050
  Fax: (021) 674 1507
  mail@stodels.com

Super Plants
• 1 Hazelden Drive
  Somerset West, 7130
  Tel: (021) 852 4992
  Fax: (021) 852 4899
  Email: somerset@superplants.co.za
• On Parklands Main Road
  Parklands, 7441
  Tel: (021) 556 8664
  Fax: (021) 556 8669
  Email: parklands@superplants.co.za
• 1 Link Road
  Bothasig, 7441
  Tel: (021) 558 0190
  Fax: (021) 558 5413
  Email: bothasig@superplants.co.za
• On Tokai Main Road
  Tokai, 7441
  Tel: (021) 715 4666
  Fax: (021) 713 1569
  Email: tokai@superplants.co.za
• Corner of R43 and Main Road
  Sandbaai, Hermanus
  Tel: (028) 316 4006
  Email: hermanus@superplants.co.za

KWAZULU-NATAL

Kingfisher Creek Garden Centre
69 Torquay Avenue, Bluff, 4052
Tel: (031) 466 2112
Fax: (031) 466 3777

Top Crop Nursery
Albert Falls - 25 km from
Pietermaritzburg on Greytown Road
Tel: (033) 569 1333
Fax: (033) 569 1336
Email: topcrop@intekom.co.za
www.superlawn.co.za

MPUMALANGA

Witbank Garden Centre
24 Louise Street
Tel: (013) 697 2264

NORTH WEST PROVINCE

Hexriver Garden Centre
70 Heystek Street Rustenburg
Tel: (014) 592 3711
Fax: (014) 592 3711

EASTERN CAPE

Bloomingdales
145 Main Road, Walmer
Tel: (041) 581 5117
Email: bloomingdale@mweb.co.za

GAUTENG

Plant Land – Acacia
Old Brits Road (R513)
Rosslyn
Tel: (012) 549 4945

FREE STATE

Greenside Nursery
18 Tafelberg Avenue, Langenhovenpark
Tel: (051) 451 1164
Fax: (051) 451 1594
Email: green@intekom.co.za

Index